T0114765

PRAYING IN GOD'S WILL

DISCUSSION GUIDE

MORGAN KIZER

WESTBOW
P R E S S®
A DIVISION OF THOMAS NELSON
& ZONDERVAN

WestBow Press books may be ordered through booksellers or by contacting:

WestBow Press
A Division of Thomas Nelson & Zondervan
1663 Liberty Drive
Bloomington, IN 47403
www.westbowpress.com
844-714-3454

Cover art provided by Ella Fortenberry, a high school student at
Carmel Christian School, Matthews, North Carolina.

ISBN: 978-1-6642-9370-0 (sc)
ISBN: 978-1-6642-9369-4 (e)

Print information available on the last page.

WestBow Press rev. date: 06/15/2023

CONTENTS

ACKNOWLEDGEMENTS

I take personal responsibility for all errors and shortcomings. I HAVE and will make mistakes. the Good LORD doesn't!

This book is dedicated to Rev. Benjie Spears, who began the Calvary Church Singles Growth Groups. These groups attracted many attendees from various Christian backgrounds and resulted in positive Christian growth. Today some 45 years later the results are evident. Numerous missionaries and Christian workers and many improved and changed lives have resulted from his efforts. Thank you Benjie!

FIRST THINGS FIRST

God's will is the most important topic there is. This series of books is designed to encourage and help the reader to gain a better awareness and understanding of God's will. Above all the reader is encouraged to be constantly in God's will. In order to do God's will one needs to discover what His will is. Everything that anyone needs to know about God's will is found in The Holy Bible; follow it as the Holy Book that it is. **Prayer is the believer's communication link with the Almighty**.

A guided discussion is not the only method of teaching this material. These questions are not the only questions. My responses are not the only responses to the questions. Use the discussion/ lecture method that best fits both you and your class. However, it should be noted that when a person is guided to answer well-crafted questions they will more readily accept a point of view that they previously didn't hold or hold as firmly.

Write some of your own questions. Take notes. You may need to lead this class again. The main goal of this class is to elevate the importance of praying in God's will in the individual's daily life. Hopefully, when the class finishes this course, the student's prayer life will have improved. When a person becomes aware that a much greater percentage of their prayers are answered, their faith will be strengthened and they will be more likely to become a more effective Christian doing the assignments that the good LORD has given them.

The discussion questions and comments are designed to serve multiple purposes. They can be used as thought-provoking tools for meditating on God's will. The probing questions will aid the teacher in determining where each student is spiritually. It is hoped that each student will participate in the discussion. The shy ones will need to be given some of the more obvious questions to answer or in some cases they might participate by raising their hands in a group response. The more enthusiastic students will carry the conversation and will often need to be moderated. Until the class gets use to this format, it may be necessary to call on specific individuals to answer specific questions. This course will enable the student to go beyond the level of the text "Praying in God's Will". The readers who carefully and prayerfully studies it should gain a better prospective of prayer and why some prayers are answered and why some prayers can't be answered.

The lessons in this course can be readily used for most age groups and various predicaments. Prayer applies to very believer. While the course is divided into 30 separate lesson plans it may be wise to expand them as the enthusiasm grows.

Some of the questions are geared for a show of hands or a verbal response from the class. Others are thought provoking questions that are given to encourage the student toward thinking deeper about God's will. Some questions are used as probes to determine where the student is spiritually. A few questions are asked more than once. They can be asked twice; once or none of the questions can be used. It is always the teacher's choice. The teacher should get to know his or her class and determined the questions and statements that best fit their needs.

NOTE: The more you can get the class to discuss the topics at hand the better. Once you get the conversation started your job is to **listen**. When someone gets off track hopefully you will notice and will be able to cite a Scripture that will correct any error that may have crept in. When the students stop getting something out of the lessons, they will find other things that they think they need to do. Keep them involved and make the discussion as interesting as possible.

Sometimes a question is asked that seems to be out of sequence. These unanticipated questions are placed where they are in order to help keep the students alert and to shift the subtopics. At times, there will be a devastating local event, a tragedy, a sickness, an emotional event or other dominating incident that should be included as part of the class discussion. As gently as you can, consider weaving in appropriate prayers and Scripture verses. Prayer is relevant in all situations!

Included are thought-provoking statements. Sometimes they are in the form of a question, other times they may be a verse, and sometimes they could be just a deeper thought. When you have time to study and prepare the lesson you should come up with some thought provoking statements that apply to the lesson. These can be used in a variety of ways depending on your time restraints. Ideally, the class can use them as a homework assignment, or as something to think about before the next class meets. You might decide to open each session by giving the class some time to share their thoughts on some of the previous materials. Use your time wisely!

A CD with Power Point cited scripture verses is purposefully not provided for the course. The students are asked to lookup the verses in their own Bibles. They will by repetition learn where more books of the Bible are located. Words that are written in *italics* are not to be read to the students they are only for the teacher!

Special care has been used in the selection of pronouns that are used when the discussion is about characteristics that are unique to believers. Many times instead of using we, our, etc. a more exact word was chosen. This was done so that a non-believer who was reading the statement would not wrongly assume that he was a believer when he wasn't. Even though this avoidance might sometimes seem awkward it was done for a good reason. Throughout the book the term "believer" is given preference to the word "Christian". This is because in some cultures the word Christian is used instead of saying European, Westerner, or American.

When you are leading a guided discussion its purpose is to help the participants form solid based Biblical conclusions. The more they talk on the topics at hand the better. Should a local or personal need occur to someone in the group exercise good judgement. If you can, address the problem from the Bible. For this reason, I SUGGEST

USING A THOMPSON CHAIN REFERENCE BIBLE. When you get use to using it, you will be able to quickly find the verses that address most problems and concerns. At any time, you feel it would help, either pray or ask on of the students to pray. It is better to help a student with one of his or her needs or concerns than it is to complete every lesson on time. A Listing of the Scripture verses use in "Praying in God's Will" is provided at the end of each chapter.

NOTE: It is not necessary for you to agree with me. I could be wrong on some points. No one is perfect. Many of my comments are of a general nature; they do not always apply to everyone and every situation. My comments are provided as an aide. Reading each one to the class will make it a very boring and short-lived class. Their main use should be for the times where you didn't have an opportunity to adequately prepare the lessons for your class. Use the brain that the Good LORD gave you and follow His Spirit. Whatever He says, do it.

NOTE: Some chapters naturally lend themselves toward more discussions and others have fewer concepts to discuss. For this reason, some chapters are combined with other chapters for one discussion lesson. For example: chapter 2 and chapter 3. The volume of their discussions does not diminish their value.

CHAPTER 1

INTRODUCTION

1. **How many of you pray with some regularity?** *This is part of a series of questions to break the ice and encourage the students to open up. If someone chooses not to respond don't call them out. Let them join the discussion at their own rate and at a time of their own choosing.*

2. **How many of you have a special time for prayer?**

3. **What do you think most people pray about?** *By asking the question this way you are not putting anyone on the spot.*

4. **Did someone teach you how to pray or was it something that evolved over a period of time?** *If no one taught them and they just caught on to praying by instinct, there is always the possibility of them having incorrect beliefs and practices about prayer. NOTE: Even some very good believers have misconceptions about prayer. The devout ones are reading their Bible and are more open to Biblically based improvements.*

5. **What is prayer? Who do you pray to? The Holy Spirit, Mary, God the Father, Jesus, or a saint? In general terms what are the topics you pray about the most?** *These are set up questions for the next series of questions. These are very important!*

6. **What percentage of a normal believer's prayers, do you think, are clearly answered? Think about what your percentage of answered prayers are.** What part of these are answered in the affirmative? You made a request and you clearly received the answer that you requested? (When the answer is **NO,** it is an answered prayer.)

7. **Why do you think some of the "unanswered" requests were unanswered?** *Note the people who blame God verses the ones who take the responsibility themselves.*

8. **The context of this book is from a Christian perspective. What do you think qualifies a person to be a Christian?** (*Be prepared to lead someone down the Roman Road:* Romans 3:23,6:23, 5:8, 10: 9, 10, and 13. *Should the Spirit move you*)

9. **Who do you think God expects to live a holy life?** *Any answer less than every believer is deficient.*

10. **How would you describe a person who is living a holy life?** One whose presents motivates me toward holiness. He would also be someone who was up-to-date in his forgiveness prayers and Scripture readings.

11. **Do holy people sin? If so, what do they do about it?** Everyone on earth sins! The holier one is, the less frequent they sin and the quicker they ask the Father for His forgiveness.

12. **Have someone read Romans 7:14-25 then discuss the old and new nature that is present in all believers.** The old nature moves you toward sin while the new nature moves you toward holiness. **What determines the one that you listen to?** The one you feed the most!

13. **How does a person nourish their old nature?** By small compromises with others who are sinning, by giving in to small temptations, by not keeping up-to-date in confessing your sins to the Father, etc. **It is very easy to slip into this mode where you are not daily reading and mediating on the Word!**

14. **How does a person nourish their new nature?** By studying God's Word, by praying regularly, by attending worship services and prayer meetings; but most of all, by choosing moment by moment to live the holy life that the Holy Spirit leads you to live.

15. **How can a person know which of his natures he is nourishing?** By constantly reading and studying the Holy Bible and keeping up-to-date with his forgiveness prayers!

16. **How can a believer have proper standing so that he can correctly communicate with the Almighty?** By sincerely praying forgiveness prayers for the sins that they have committed. The quicker you do this after becoming aware of sinning, the better! *The person who is not aware of committing any sins is in very deep trouble!*

17. **How do people become aware of their sins?** That is the Holy Spirits function. Satan also makes people aware of their sins even after they have asked for forgiveness. **Why does he do this?** He wants believers to feel guilty even after they have been forgiven so that they will live a defeated life.

18. **What's wrong with a believer telling God how he would like Him to handle a specific problem?** He is much smarter than we are. His solution is always the best. It is a very common human weakness to forget that the LORD is infinitely smarter than we are. It is one thing to tell Him about our problems and ask Him to handle them. It is another to tell Him how He should handle them. Most, if not all, of the things that we need are not desired by our old sin nature!

19. **Why is it so difficult for a believer to trust the good LORD to make the best choices for him and to protect him from harm?** We know that He loves us and we know that He communicates the best choices for us, yet, we still have a problem trusting the LORD. It is always a faith deficiency.

20. **Ask someone to read Luke 11:1-4.** Discuss the various points that are covered in the ideal prayer.

21. **Read Matthew chapter 6 verses 5-15**. *(Pause after each verse and discuss the elements of prayer that are recorded there.)*

22. **What is the one legitimate sincere heart felt prayer that any non-believer can pray and receive a positive answer.** "Dear God, please forgive me of my sins and save me from the eternal penalty of my sins."

23. **What is one of the most prolific false beliefs regarding salvation.** That it can be earned by doing good works! **Salvation is not based on good works (being good). This belief is very common and is also a false belief!!!)** It has crept into many denominations and is embraced by cults.

> **"For by grace you have been saved through**
> **faith. And this is not your own**
> **doing: it is the gift of God, not a result of**
> **works, so that no one may boast."**
> Ephesians 2:8-9

Chapter 1 in "Praying in God's Will"

INEFFECTIVE PRAYERS

WHAT SHOULD I PRAY ABOUT

1. **Are there prayers that the good LORD doesn't want to hear?**
   Yes, Prayers that try to justify or in some way promote sin.
   NOTE: There is a great difference between asking the Father
   for something and telling Him what He needs to do!

2. **What kind of prayers are never answerable?** Those that are
   dishonest and those that are just voiced and not meant. Even
   a very pious prayer that many saints have prayed will not be
   answered if the one praying it doesn't mean what he or she is
   saying.

3. **Does the Bible have anything to say about selfish prayers?**
   What kind of help is available to a believer so that he can pray
   better prayers?

> "Likewise the Spirit helps us in our weakness. For we do not know what to pray for as we ought, but the Spirit himself intercedes for us with groanings too deep for words."
>
> Romans 8:26

4. **Why shouldn't we pray for <u>all</u> the missionaries to be effective and <u>all</u> the sick people to get well?** There are non- and anti-Christian groups who have recruiters that they call missionaries, everyone eventually dies. We don't want to be praying against God's will.

5. **How can a regular person know Gods will?** By Studying His Word!

> "Thy word is a lamp unto my feet, and a light unto my Path."
>
> Psalms 119 vs. 105 KJV

6. **What are some of the things a believer can in good conscience pray for?** For the salvation of lost people, for wisdom, for guidance, and for God's will to be done.

7. **What are some of the things a believer can in good conscience pray against?** Anything that the Word condemns. Any actions that anyone is doing or planning to do that are contrary to the Word.

Verse	Chapter	Page	Topic
Matthew 6:7	2	10	Pray honestly and concisely.
Romans 8:26	2	10	Functions of the Holy Spirit
(James 4:3)	2	10	Unanswered prayers

8. **How would you describe the new nature that a person receives when he becomes a believer?** It is the part of the believer's spirit that supports and obeys the active works of the Holy Spirit in the believer. He gets this nature when he becomes a believer. It leads the person toward righteous thoughts and actions.

9. **What kind of things promote your old nature?** Giving in to what we might call very small sins and choices that make temptation more accessible. These "small sins" tend to escalate quickly into much worse sins.

10. **What kind of things promote the new nature that you received when you became a believer?** Bible study, prayer, worship, Christian fellowship, following the leading of the Holy Spirit and the teachings of God's Word.

11. **Why is it so important to stress the concept of the new nature and the old nature?** It is taught in the Bible. It is important for every believer to know and understand why they occasionally sin and how to reduce this occurrence by nurturing their new nature. When one doesn't understand this concept, they are in a downward series of events. Many may think that they might have lost their salvation. Paul had the same problems with his old nature that we do.

12. **How often can you distinguish which nature someone else is operating under?** As often as the Holy Spirit quickens you. When you see another believer commit or start to commit a sin that you have been forgiven of or have read about in the Scripture it will be very apparent. **NOTE: No one but the good LORD can or has the right to judge another believer! However, each believer should be ready to offer Scriptural advice when the Spirit moves him to do so.**

13. **Why it is often very difficult for a believer to distinguish which nature is influencing him toward a specific activity?** A sever lack of Bible familiarity and a void of forgiveness prayers. If a person is in fact a believer, the Holy Spirit living in them will convict and guide them, if He hasn't been quenched. When this happens, He will sometime let you suffer the earthly consequences of sin until you are driven to repent.

14. **From time-to-time non-believers do something that we perceive is good. What do you think was their motivation?** Pride! Many times, the unbeliever thinks that he can go to heaven by doing good works. (see Ephesians 2:8&9)

15. **When the opportunity to do something that is definitely good and Biblical arises, how do you determining whether or not it is God's will for you to do it?** You pray and ask the LORD for guidance. The more you do God's will the more familiar you will become with the areas that He wants you to function in. At one time or another each of us will also be asked to function outside of our gifting. God's grace is sufficient! Some of the good things are reserved for others to do.

16. **How can you test the Spirits in order to make the right response?** You compare the spirits leadings with the written Word. The Holy Spirit will always be in agreement with the Bible!

17. **Can a believer make the correct decision in a matter for the wrong reasons? If he determines this later on what should he do about it?** Yes. If a believer determines that he has made a wrong and irreversible decision, what should he do about it? Repent and resolve to increase his Bible study and prayer time. It is always good to pray that you will become more sensitive to the voice of the Holy Spirit!

18. **When a believer finds it necessary to make a decision about what he should do in order to determine the LORD's will in a matter. What else should he do?** Make it a prayer priority and study the Scriptures that reflect on the topic. *(A very good reason for having a Thompson Chain Reference Bible.)* Regardless of what the decision is the believer can always commit the outcome to the good LORD! The LORD has no problems with making course corrections for us. Some of these are definitely not the choices we would naturally choose to make!

19. **What advice could you give to a very young child about making good decisions?** Pray and ask Jesus to help you make the right decision. Generally speaking, you should tell them to obey their parents. **THERE ARE SOME VERY RARE EXCEPTIONS!**

20. **What is the best prayer to pray when you are considering a decision?** Pray that God's will is done and ask for the guidance of the Holy Spirit. Note: Sometimes the LORD guides the believer to another person who has the knowledge, gifting and experience level that enables him to offer good practical advice.

21. **Should a believer lay out a fleece in order to make a correct decision?** Signs were promised to the Jews. You may or may not receive a sign. Pray for wisdom and read your Bible for additional instructions. In some cases, it is appropriate to go to a Spiritual leader that you trust, a pastor, elder, deacon, a Sunday School teacher etc. and ask them to help you with the decision. The best of these will direct you to a special Scripture verse. You will not always receive an instant answer because the LORD sometimes chooses to build your patience.

22. **What can you do if you can't get a clear enough direction?**
You commit the decision to the good LORD and jump in, only
when you have to, and trust Him for redirections. Most of the
time it is appropriate to simply wait on the LORD. Sometimes
you are specifically instructed to just wait. Other times there may
seem to be an empty void. If so fill it with heart felt Scripture
readings and prayer. Waiting on the LORD is far more difficult
than most people realize. Scriptures tell us to abide in Christ.

> **"Abide in me, and I in you. As the branch**
> **cannot bear fruit by itself,**
> **unless it abides in the vine, neither can**
> **you, unless you abide in me."**
>
> John 15:4

Verse	*Chapter*	*Page*	*Topic*
I Chronicles 29:13	3	17	Thank God
Psalms 17:6	3	20	God answers.
Psalm 52:8-9KJV	3	17	God's steadfast love
Psalms 54:2	3	20	God hears.
Psalms 55:1-2	3	20	God listens.
Psalms 75:1	3	18	Give thanks
Psalm 100:1-5KJV	3	17	Thanksgiving
Psalms 102:1-2	3	21	God listens.
Psalms 103:11-12	3	15	God forgives
Psalms 105:3-5	3	16	Give glory to God.
Psalm 107:1-2KJV	3	18	Give thanks.
Psalms 113:1-4	3	18	Praise God.
Psalm 117 1-2KJV	3	18	Praise God.

Psalms 139:23-24KJV	3	14	Search me O God.
Psalms 143:10KJV	3	19	God teaches.
Proverbs 24 9KJV	3	13	The thought of foolishness is sin.
Isaiah 43:25KJV	3	15	God blots out forgiven sins.
Jeremiah 29:11-14a	3	15	God's plans
Jeremiah 33:3	3	15	Call on God.
Ezekiel 3:18-19KJV	3	14	Warn the wicked
Amos 5:4	3	16	Seek God and live.
Matthew 8:5b-7	3	19	Jesus heals.
Matthew 12:50	3	19	Doing God's will
Luke 4:38-39	3	20	Jesus heals.
Luke 11:2 KJV	3	19	Thy will be done.
John 4:46-47	3	20	Jesus heals.
(John 16:7-8)	3	14	The Holy Spirit convicts sinners.
John 16:24	3	21	Ask
(Romans 3:23)	3	13	All have sinned.
Romans 8:26-27	3	21	Functions of the Holy Spirit
I Corinthians 15:56-57	3	18	Victory over sin
Ephesians 1:7-8	3	15	God forgives.
James 5:13-16	3	22	Proof of faith
I John 1:9	3	14	Confess sins

CHAPTER 4

HEALING PRAYERS FOR YOURSELF AND OTHERS

1. **Do you as a believer think that you must have the spiritual gift of healing in order to pray an effective prayer for a sick person to get well**? A believer can pray in good conscious for any good thing. Any believer, who has sincerely asked the good LORD to forgive him of his sins, is able and qualified to pray a worthwhile "first aid" prayer for any godly purpose. The LORD always chooses when and how to answer. Some believers have a much better answer rate than others. Ask yourself, Why. Perhaps they are pursuing the holy life more seriously and are submerged deeper in the Word.

2. **Do you know of anyone who has been healed?** At one time or another each of us has been sick. We got well! We will never know this side of Heaven what part the good LORD played in our cure. We should always thank Him for every blessing we receive. We should also thank Him for the bad things that could have happened but didn't!

3. **Have you ever been sick? Are you still sick? How did you get well? What part of your getting well is due to the good LORD? The underlying question is why does the LORD allow anyone to get sick?** There are many reasons. Sometimes a person gets sick because he or she did things that are unhealthy. Or as in the case of exercise and good nutrition, they didn't do what they knew they should. The LORD can use sickness to get our attention. He can use sickness to detour us in our earthly journey. He may use sickness as a demonstration of His power. HE KNOWS WHAT HE IS DOING! How can He heal someone, if they didn't get sick? NOTE: Because of Adam's sin in the garden of Eden the earth was cursed. Part of this curse is sickness. What we should consider is that a little sin can have vast repercussions and cause much suffering.

4. **Do you believe that all of the LORD's healings are instantly done?** No! Some are done over a period of time. Sometimes, He uses doctors, nurses, pastors, elders, and Christian friends in the process. An instant healing is done for a very good and rare reason. He is the only one who knows exactly why.

5. **How does the Scripture address the topic of being healthy?** Scriptures contain dietary rules and mentions some activities that are beneficial for the body. Scriptures contain sanitation guidelines and other good health related advice. Scriptures also contain recipes for some foods. **I.e., Ezekiel bread, LOOK IT UP!** (Ezekiel 4:9)

6. **How many of these health-related topics can you name and how many of them can you find in the Bible?** You might think about the word, "Kosher", meaning clean.

7. **Do you think that Jesus was ever sick? Yes! - NO!** Scripture is not clear on this matter. Many people believe that He was never sick. We do know that he had problems according to Isaiah 53 1-12. He definitely knew what sickness was.

8. **Can you name an event that drives people to pray desperately any more that a severe health problem? REPHRASED, what are the spiritual reasons why people get sick?** Sickness is a reminder that our stay on earth is just temporary. Don't waste your time. Use it wisely!

9. **What are some of the benefits of being sick?** Sickness promotes prayer. Both you and others pray for improvements in your condition. The good Lord has no problem getting our attention. In sickness our ability to have empathy with others who are sick also can be increased

10. **What should you do for a sick or injured friend?** You can always pray for the good LORD to be merciful to them. You can also help them with daily living tasks. Get their mail, feed and walk their dog, cat, bird, fish etc. Sometimes they might need a ride to see a doctor. Other times they will want to talk with someone. There are times when they will want to be left alone so that they can rest. If you don't know, you can always ask. If you are sick, ask your friends to help you but don't take advantage of them. If possible rotate the request among them so that you will not overburden any one person.

11. **Why do people die?** It's the LORD's way of saying that they have finished their earthly assignments. Sometimes it is because He doesn't want them to do any more harm to His name.

12. **In II Kings chapter 5 it speaks about Naaman. What details of his story tend to latch on to you? What elements of this story are relevant to you?** Never forget the kindness of the little servant girl. She was a slave but she chose to do something good for her master. Have you prayed for your boss?

13. **What lessons should we learn from the little servant girl?** Believers should do good things for everyone that they come in contact with. Others will see the difference in our lives. Some will turn to God. Some may become our friends.

14. **In your opinion what are some of the reasons why many people are sick?** Some people get sick because the LORD wants to get their attention and other times it is to stop some behaviors. Sickness is part of life. Everyone from time to time needs to stop and think, pray, and be thankful.

15. **How does a non-believer handle sickness?** Most handle it with dread and many react poorly.

16. **How should a believer react to illness?** He should pray and ask other believers to pray for him. The believer should pray for his doctors and nurses. Sometimes he will meet another patient who needs prayer. It is not necessary to announce or even ask permission to pray silently for another person. Sometimes a believer will be used to chat with someone in the hospital or doctor's office. If so, you may be led to shift the conversation to a more spiritual line of thought. Oftentimes, the presents of a Bible on your tray stand will make a statement. If you are in the hospital, always ask for a chaplain visit! They may be liberal; they may be of another faith but ask. **<u>When people stop asking there will be fewer chaplains.</u>**

17. **If someone is sick and desires to be Divinely healed what should he be doing toward this end?** Everyone who is sick should use the occasion to ask the good LORD to forgive them of their sins. A believer should always notify his church and his pastor and ask for prayers. Sickness can be a very soul-searching event. If you are a member of a Sunday school class, you should let them know. They will pray for you and provide more help than anyone else. NOTE: Some sicknesses are very personal. You don't have to spell out every detail. It should suffice to let them know that you are sick and having health problems.

"Is anyone among you sick? Let him call for the elders of the church, and let them pray over him, anointing him with oil in the name of The LORD. And the prayer of faith will save the one who is sick, and The LORD will raise him up. And if he has committed sins, he will be

forgiven. Therefore confess your sins to one another and pray for one another, that you may be healed. The prayer of a righteous person has great power as it is working."

James 5:14-16

18. **What event should be more important to a sick person than being healed, if any?** Someone becoming a new believer. This includes the sick person. For a believer to become more holy.

19. **The first 12 apostles definitely had the Spiritual gift of healing. Under what circumstances did they have problems healing a sick person?** Some conditions require more than just a healing prayer. They require prayer and fasting.

20. **How should a believer react if someone that is close by is suddenly injured? If you are the one who is injured? Do you pray about a person being healed from an injury any differently from a person who is sick?** Some injuries are evidently so serious that any reasonable person would realize that the injured person only has a few seconds left. In these cases, the believer hast to be instantly ready and spiritually equipped with the Word to act as the LORD leads him to act. In a true

emergency there will be no time to look up a verse or to pray for personal forgiveness. You could be in the dark or there might not be a Bible available. Should you pray for an evil person to be healed? If so, is this prayer any different from a prayer you might offer for the healing of a devout believer?

21. **What should you do if the person dies?** BE RESPECTFUL.

Verse	Chapter	Page	Topic
(II Kings ch. 5)	4	24	Naaman's story
II Kings 5:14	4	24	Naaman is healed.
Isaiah 53:5 KJV	4	23	Jesus heals.
(John 9:1-7)	4	25	A reason for sickness.
Hebrews 9:27	4	27	Everyone dies.
James 5:14-16	4	27	Healing prayer

THE SCOPE OF OUR PRAYERS

WHERE SHOULD WE PRAY

1. **Should the content of our prayers be detailed or should it be in general terms?**

NB: Not even the best of believers has any business telling the all-knowing Creator of the Universe how He should or needs to do anything! Honestly express your needs and concerns. Next, your prayer should contain a request that the good LORD take over the outcome of the situation, problem or need in the way that He thinks is best. He knows much better than we can imagine what the best solution is to any problem. The best underlying thought to any prayer should always be that His will is done. There is nothing better!

2. **Would it be dishonest to want something good and not pray for it?** Yes, but keep in mind that the good LORD may have something even better in the works. Most likely it is something that could help you to become more holy. Our old sin nature

doesn't like anything that leads us toward holiness. NOTE: Sometimes the something that is better is hard to recognize and accept.

3. **Should a believer put an overriding condition on their prayers? i.e.,** That if the request is outside of Gods will that the LORD will do whatever is in His will. This add-on, when it is sincere and honest makes your prayer answerable, in the affirmative. You ask for God's will to be done, and you get His will. What more should you want? Jesus gave us the example, in the Garden of Gethsemane. See **Matthew 26:36-39.**

4. **When someone is sick and ask for prayer, how do you pray for them?** Your prayer should indicate that you trust your heavenly Father to do the best possible thing. You can always ask for His mercy. If the person has specific conditions that need to be addresses it is appropriate that you pray that the Good LORD handle that condition i.e., temperature, blood pressure, bleeding etc.

5. **What do you think is a good by-product of having more of your prayers answered?** That both your faith and the faith of the people that you prayed for will increase.

6. **When you have many items that you want to pray about should they be in any particular order? What should be the determining factor?** The leading of the Holy Spirit should always be the first priority! Always be honest and sincere in your prayers. Even then, sometimes in trying to do so, you will ask for things that the LORD knows will be bad for you. Therefore, by asking that the LORDs will be done is the best factor to include in a prayer. It makes your prayer answerable. NOTE: Your old sin nature will probably not like His answer!

7. **If a stranger were to ask you to pray for their need would you feel obligated to pray for them?** Suppose you were asked over the TV or radio? I believe that prayers should be offered for every sincere request. Not all of these prayers need to be vocal.

8. **Why should a believer be listening to the Holy Spirit when he is making a request of the Father?** Good communication, mainly listening, is important in all prayers and activities. This should be concurrent with meaningful Bible study.

---

9. **Are there physical locations where you would have difficulty praying?** Any place where there is excessive noise or sinful actives, may be difficult to pray in. If you are not there for a God honoring purpose; then, you should leave as soon as you can. No earthling is above temptation.

10. **Is there a place where you can pray without any distractions?** You can be distracted in a dark sound proof room. There is no perfect place on earth. However, there is always one accessible place that is better than the others in your environment. It might be that your best available place is to face a certain direction. The good LORD wants believers to pray. Ask Him to provide the place and conditions that He wants you to pray in. Sometimes, going to the bathroom is the best that you can do.

11. **Is it beneficial to pray totally alone just you and the Father?** Some of Jesus's prayers were preyed in desolate places, others were in very public places. Many times, it is a matter of the nature of your prayers. When you are praying for someone else especially for healing it is often good, if they can hear your prayer. If the LORD choses to heal or otherwise help them, then it will be easier for them to relate the healing to the good LORD. NOTE: Don't claim personal credit for anything that the LORD does!

12. **Some people use the term "prayer closet", as a place for special daily prayers. what do you consider the ideal place for this?** It should be as private and as quite as you can find. It may be dark or dimly lit so that you can read Scriptures during your prayer or totally dark. It may literally be in a closet.

13. **What are some of the common distractions people face when they choose to pray?** The phone rings, someone knocks at your door, A helicopter flies over your head, the dog barks, you suddenly remember something that you need to do. The answer to a problem that you have been trying to solve comes to you. The list is never ending. Just ask the good LORD to help you pray. Expect Him to act. It is called faith.

14. **Which distractions can you take care of in order to have a non-interrupted prayer time?** You can ask the LORD to direct you, then you do the reasonable things that come to mind. Perhaps you have a neighbor who is making excessive noise. Instead of calling the police, you can pray for them. No doubt they are having spiritual problems. (Who isn't?)

15. **What time do you find is most effective for your extended prayers?** It is good to have a specific schedule. It is very easy to get caught up in daily activities and skip a prayer time appointment. Pick a time that works for you. You can have more than one!

16. **Have you ever been moved to pray for someone or something out of the blue with no idea of why you need to pray for them?** *(NOTE 1: This is another way of asking if you are spiritually alert. Note 2: Sometimes a long silent pause is helpful. Normally, someone will break the silence.)*

17. **Do you prefer to pray in a dimly lit space or do you prefer to pray in total darkness?** Everyone is different. Don't push your optimum conditions on others. Let them work with the good LORD to arrange things the way that He wants them to

be. <u>Learning to identify and follow His promptings is in many cases more important than some of the other things that He may be prompting you to do!</u>

18. **Do you pray when you are driving or while going for a walk?** If you do, do you think of it as a natural expression or do you think of it as following the Scripture that says to pray without ceasing? How do you classify of your unscheduled prayers? What difference does our classifications of a prayer make?

19. **Is there a time or condition where you shouldn't be praying?** *(Notice the students that seem to be asking themselves about it.)*

20. **Is there anyone that you shouldn't be praying for?** Those who are dead. You can still thank the LORD for the good things they did. *NOTE: There are cults where volunteers are literally baptized for the dead.*

PRAYER POSTURES

PRAYER INTENSITY

1. **What are the two main types of prayer postures?** The one that is in your heart and the one that is of your body.

2. **What is the purpose of a prayer posture of your body?** It is a way of authenticating that you are not casually praying. In some circumstances, it can be a very bold statement!

3. **Why did so many people in the Bible have a prayer posture?** There are many reasons. Culturally, they were accustomed to being ruled by kings. Their kings demanded respect so they bowed before them. NOTE: Bowing is cross-cultural. It is practiced in many cultures, worldwide. It demonstrates respect. True believers also believed that God is much greater than any

earthly power. Therefore, they believed that they should show Him even greater respect. Many of them are embarrassed by the casual manner of dress that many "believers" have when attending a worship service today!

4. **What are the prayer postures that are mentioned in the Bible? To name a few:** 1.Lying flat on the ground, face down. 2. Bowing. 3. Lifting up both hands toward heaven. 4. Kneeling.

5. **What do each of them illustrate?** They demonstrate humbleness and respect for the Almighty.

6. **Why do people normally close their eyes when they pray?** To minimize some of the distractions that are always present.

7. **Are prayer postures part of a total expression of what is in your heart when you pray?** Normally, when I kneel for prayer, it is a more serious prayer.

8. **When should you not use a prayer posture?** When it would be dangerous i.e., when you are driving. When you believe that it would be considered a show by the ones around you. In either case you still have options. You can pull over at a rest stop or filling station. In a group setting you can go to the bathroom. There is always a way that you can respectfully pray. It could be that the best that you could do is to pray silently with your eyes open. Other times bold oral prayer is called for. You can always ask the good LORD to guide you.

9. **If you were called on in a public event to pray, what would discourage you from using your normal prayer posture? Where did this discouragement come from?** There are only two possibilities. The Good LORD and Satan. Pick one!

10. **What are some of the elements of a spiritual prayer posture?** Humility, sincerity, honesty, thankfulness, realizing how insignificant you are, yet you are now in the throne room of Almighty God, Creator of the universe.

11. **What other spiritual thing that you do has a posture associated with it?** Expressions of friendship can be considered a posture. i.e., waving or shaking hands. In the military coming to attention demonstrates respect.

Verse	*Chapter*	*Page*	*Topic*
Exodus 34:8	7	35	Moses bowed.
Joshua 5:14	7	35	Joshua fell on his face.
I Kings 8:54	7	35	Solomon knelt.
Matthew 26:39	7	35	Jesus fell on His face.

12. **How emotional should you get when you pray?** Prayers should always be very honest. You shouldn't inflate your emotions nor should you become more stoic. If your emotions are honest, and not part of an earthly scheme to improve your chances of getting you prayers answered favorably or to impress someone, then an honest expression is probably appreciated. If it isn't honest, the LORD is well aware of what you are trying to do.

13. **Which emotions are normally involved when you pray?** Your LOVE FOR JESUS should be the overriding emotion in every prayer.

14. **Are there occasions where you pump-up your emotions?** In emergency life or death matters it is difficult not to express your emotions. A word of caution. Don't pray granite faced to the Almighty and don't artificially pump up your feelings. The LORD knows the need and when you pray honestly for His will to be done you have prayed a more answerable prayer. **KEEP IT HONEST**!

15. **Should you pump up your emotions when you pray? How about the emotion of LOVE?** NOTE: The LORD knows when you are lying emotionally.

16. **How do you think the good LORD responds to our emotions?** Appropriately!

17. **Should public prayers recognize in any way the people who are standing near-by and no doubt listening?** Yes. Many times, in the Bible public prayers were spoken partially for the benefit of those who were present and listening to the prayer. Some things are necessarily better to pray for openly and others are better kept just between you and your heavenly Father.

18. **When you are praying about the same topic what is the difference in your prayers between when they are private and when they are public?** Private prayers are normally longer and deeper. Public prayers can also uplift some of the hearers spiritually.

19. **On the average do you think your percentage of answered prayers changes between public and private prayers?** The result is probably about the same. However, the important factor is the spiritual condition of the person who is praying. As soon as you detect that you are not being fully submissive to the Holy Spirit you should immediately pray for forgiveness. Otherwise, you shouldn't expect to be heard.

20. **When the LORD answers a public prayer do you think the answer is more likely to be a dramatic answer?** The good LORD doesn't have to hype up an answer in order for it to be effective. It is always a matter of His Spirit working in the appropriate hearts.

21. **What examples of public and private prayer can you give from the Bible?** Adam and Eve talked with God in the Garden of Eden, Solomon's prayer dedicating the temple. (Note: Adam and Eve's prayer was public because everyone in the entire world was present.)

CHAPTER 9

REPETITIVE PRAYERS – IS ONCE ENOUGH?

1. **Is it a faith deficiency when a person prays for the same thing more than once?** For some people it can be a faith deficiency. However, on the other hand, a repeated prayer can be a source of spiritual strength. It's a matter of trusting the Father regardless of changing earthly circumstances.

2. **Do you know of a prayer, in the Bible, by a true believer, where the believer prayed more than once for the same thing?** Paul prayed multiple times for his own healing. He wasn't healed. But he did get an ample supply of God's grace. (II Corinthians 12: 7-9)

3. **When should a believer pray additional prayers about the same topic?** When the Holy Spirit moves Him to. When a need is desperate and urgent most believers will pray as much as they possibly can!

4. **There are numerous stories of believers who prayed for the salvation of a specific lost person for a very long time.** Most of these stories end with the subject of their prayers coming to the LORD. **What lesson should we draw from them?** When a believer is given the calling to pray for someone's salvation, the prayers should continue until the object of their prayers either gets saved or dies. Some needs require spiritual perseverance!

5. **When a believer is persistent in a special prayer need, what lessons should he learn from them?** The LORD has gotten our attention on a spiritual matter. Most likely, this is related to one of our assignments.

6. **When a believer prays a repetitive prayer over a period of time do you think that he consistently uses the same words or do you believe that the prayer is gradually being refined?** It could go either way. However, when a person uses the same words over and over the possibility of their prayers becoming a meaningless chant becomes more likely. Believers should mean every word in their prayers. Always be honest with the LORD!

7. **If the Good LORD were to give me the answer that I am now wanting, how could it serve His purpose?** When you can't give a reasonable answer to this question, perhaps you should be praying about something else.

8. **Do you really want what you are asking for?** Satan is very skilled at putting desires into our hearts. Some of them are not evil in themselves but they are definitely distractions. Be selective in what you pray for.

9. **Why would it be God's will for you to have the answer that you are seeking?** We don't often know. However, some prayer items are obvious. Think before you ask. You can in good conscious ask the LORD to guide you in this.

10. **Could the thing that you want be outside of His will?** Regardless of how good you may think a request is, always ask that His will is done above everything else! He may have selected a later time for His answer or someone else.

11. **Is the LORD wanting you to wait for something else?** At our human best, we can only make an educated guess about the future. God knows for sure every event that will happen. When you ask Him for His will to be done you are covered on all of the bases.

12. **Could a delay be because someone else is not willing to do some critical element in His will?** Even good believers will have their earthly opinions. We will seldom know all the reasons for the actions that the good LORD takes.

13. **Is the LORD helping you to develop the virtue of patience?** We all need patience. How else do we think that we are going to get it?

14. **How does the parable found in Luke chapter 18 apply to prayer?** Verse 1 Identifies prayer as the topic.

15. **What are the benefits of a clearly answered prayer?** You are drawn closer to Christ. When your faith is increased, there will be a tendency to pray more.

16. **What do you expect the good LORD to do, if your request is outside of His will?** While we all would probably like a detailed explanation. Don't expect one. However, you may be led to study a specific part of the Scriptures. I would hope that the good LORD would show me more clearly that the requested result was outside of His will and that I could learn from my error.

17. **Sometimes when are we being impatient we will pray another prayer for something that we have already prayed for?** Under what conditions should we pray for the same thing multiple times? When we are convenience that the solution to the need is in God's will.

18. **Why are multiple prayers sometimes necessary?** Sometimes we are obsessed with an idea and the LORD wants us to think about it in depth. Other times we are exercising stubbornness. **How can we discover what is driving us?**

19. **What is the difference between stubbornness and perseverance?** Stubbornness is we are compelled to seek our will. Perseverance is when we are striving to do God's will.

20. **What is the reason God created us?** For fellowship with Him? Prayer is one of the ways we can fellowship with the Almighty. Prayer should normally be a joyous occasion.

21. **How does a believer fellowship with the Almighty?** By prayer, by doing the things that He created us for, and by being His obedient hands and feet in a sinful world.

Verse	*Chapter*	*Page*	*Topic*
Joshua 10:12-14	9	43	Joshua prayed & the LORD acted.
Ecclesiastes 5:2-3	9	40	Be concise.
Matthew 6:7-8	9	40	Don't use empty phrases.
Matthew 23:14 KJV	9	40	Woe to scribes and Pharisees.
(Luke 18)	9	41	The persistent pleas of a widow.
Hebrews 11:6	9	41	Without faith

CHAPTER 10

WHEN DOES THE FATHER CHOOSE TO ANSWER PRAYERS?

PRAYERS THAT ARE ALWAYS ANSWERED

1. **Since some prayers are set into motion before we ask (Isaiah 65:24). Then why do we need to ask Him?** He wants us to ask Him things so that we will know where the answer came from. He knows when we are going to ask Him something. Since some of His answers take time to fulfill, He starts the process early so that we receive what He wants us to have when He wants us to have it. Answered prayers tend to build faith! NOTE 1: It takes time when he chooses to use other humans to do something related to our need. Just as we are often slow to respond to His will so are many of them

2. Sometimes, if not often, the good LORD answers our prayers and we are not aware of it. **Why are we not aware of His answers?** We probably were not looking for an answer and too often we are absorbed in worldly activities. A faith deficiency!

3. **Should we keep a written list of our prayer requests?** If a need is truly important, we will be concerned about it every time we pray. It is not our job to grade the Almighty! But a reminder of answered prayers can tend to build faith.

4. **How can we improve on our awareness of what the LORD is doing??** When we pray we should pause and listen spiritually for a few minutes. When we are not praying we should be alert to our environment for any incoming activities that He wants us to see. If we don't truly believe that He is going to answer our request, we will not be looking for His answer. He is the one who decides how He is going to communicate with us. NOTE: God has already communicated most of His answers to us. It is called the Holy Bible. It is up to us to read it!

5. **What should a believer do when the Father gives him an answer that he doesn't like?** We should embrace His answers and ask for His help so that we can understand better what He is teaching us. The LORD doesn't make any casual decisions nor does He make any mistakes.

6. **What do you think is the LORD's number one reason for the answers that He gives us?** He wants more than anything else for us to be **HOLY!**

7. **Name some prayers that are always appropriate.** Prayers for forgiveness, prayers for salvation, prayers of thanksgiving, prayers of praise, and prayers for God's will to be done.

8. In the book of Deuteronomy Moses pleaded with God to allow him to enter the promise land. The LORD responded:

    "Enough from you; do not speak to me of this matter again."
    Deuteronomy 3:26b.

    We can easily criticize Moses for praying for something where the LORD had said NO. **But are we sensitive enough to hear His No's for us and stop asking for things outside of His will? What do you think some of His reasons are for saying NO**? He understands the end result of our request. Too many times our request spring from our old sin nature. It just keeps raising its ugly head.

9. **Can you name someone else who didn't get what he prayed for? Jesus!** Jesus' prayer in Gethsemane **Matthew 26:39-44** When He was facing a terrible death on the cross He asked if

possible that the Father would spare Him. Nevertheless, **He gave believers the example that they should always ask that the Father override our wants in favor of His will being done!** (These verses are a very difficult lesson for the name it and claim it crowd!)

10. **What are the circumstances where two or more believers can agree on something and the good LORD will answer their request?** When two Christians have a disagreement and together they decide on a good solution to their dispute the good LORD will support their unity; provided that their request is fully scriptural.

11. **How do some Christians misuse this verse?**

> **"Again I say to you, if two of you agree**
> **on earth about anything**
> **they ask, it will be done for them by my Father in heaven."**
>
> Matthew 18:19

They mistakenly believe that they can ask anything, even unbiblical request and because they ganged up on the good LORD and quoted a verse they think that He will have to do their bidding. The LORD doesn't have to do anything!

Verse	_Chapter_	_Page_	_Topic_
Deuteronomy 3:26b	10	47	Unanswerable prayers
Isaiah 65:24)	10	45	God answers before you ask.
(Matthew 18:15)	10	47	sins against you
Matthew 18:19	10	47	When two or three agree
II Corinthians 12:8-9a	10	47	God's grace is sufficient.

12. **Using your best guess – What percentage of your prayers are clearly answered by the Father? What percentage of normal believers are aware of His answers? Are some prayers unanswerable? Why? NOTE:** When His answer is NO! It is an answered prayer! The answer to both questions is the same for most people. It is embarrassingly low! The reason is simple: There is excessive unconfessed unrepentant sin in our lives along with a severe faith deficiency!

13. **Can you name at least three sincere heart felt prayers that are always answered, in the affirmative:**
    a. Dear LORD please forgive me of my sins, save me from the eternal punishment that I deserve, and let me live forever with you in heaven.
    b. Dear LORD please forgive me of a specific sin.
    c. Dear LORD may your will be done.

14. **Are there others?** I once heard a pastor[14] say in a sermon that any Believer could pray and ask the Father what he should

be doing that would bring the most honor to the Father and that this was an always answered prayer. I tend to agree with him. (1 Cor. 10:31, Col 3:17) In my way of thinking this is a subcategory of asking for God's will to be done. Some people misunderstand why God expects us to give Him honor, praise, glory etc. for doing something. It is not an ego factor!!!! He wants us to know Him! The more we understand Him and the more we understand His will, the better off we will be.

15. **Why are some answers difficult for us to accept?** We are all sinners and most of the time our old nature is strongly influencing us.

16. **What should a good believer do when he gets an answer to a heartfelt prayer that he doesn't like or understand?** When you have a problem accepting His answer, you have a spiritual problem that requires attention. Ask the Father to help you embrace His will. Ask Him to lead you to a Scripture verse that sheds additional light on what His will is. Sometimes we may mis-label one of Satan's interferences as God's answer. Most of the time, we are rebellious and out of fellowship with the Father. On our human homemade scale of measuring, we may count our rebellion as a small insignificant amount. A small amount rebellion (sin) goes a long way!

17. **Why is it important for us to get an affirmative answer to our prayers?** Each affirmative positive answer tends to build our faith!

> **"But without faith it is impossible to please Him: for he that cometh to God must believe that he is, and that he is a rewarder of them that diligently seek him."**
> Hebrews 11:6 KJV

18. **When we get affirmative positive answers to our prayers what does this tell us?** Our current relationship with the Father is likely in good working order.

19. **How do we build on this?** We continue to read the Bible, and pray for God's will to be done. We should also put forth an effort not to get spiritually big headed over it.

20. **What should we do about the things that we want and apparently can't have?** We can ask the Father to help us deal with our wants.

21. **What do you expect to happen when God says NO! And we keep on praying for the same thing?** Stubbornness has a price! Sometimes He gives us exactly what we asked for and then we are plagued with all the problems that it brings.

Verse	_Chapter_	_Page_	_Topic_
(Ezra 7: 10, 18)	11	49	God's will is done!
Hebrews 11:6bKJV	11	50	Faith is imperative.
I John 5: 14-15KJV	11	49	Praying in God's will

CHAPTER 12

HINDRANCES TO PRAYER

1. **Name some hindrances to prayer that you are aware of.**
   The phone rings, someone knocks at the door, the dog barks,
   something important comes to mind that you need to write
   down. The list is endless.

2. **What do you think is the greatest hindrance to prayer?** The
   sin of pride. The casual thought that I don't need to pray is
   always a major celebration for Satan.

3. **What can you do to either eliminate or reduce prayer
   hinderances?** You can schedule your prayer for a time that you
   think might have fewer interruptions, you can turn the phone
   off, depending on how your dog reacts you might try patting
   him on the head or let him lay down by you when you pray.
   One of the most important things you can do is to ask to good
   LORD to take care of the interruptions.

4. **Is it always necessary to close your eyes when you pray? When is this not necessary?** There are circumstances where you need to be alert to your surroundings. It is part of your "pray without ceasing prayers". For example, when you are driving.

5. **Where do you think prayer distractions come from?** There is only one ultimate source, Satan!

6. **When you identify that a hindrance was sent your way by Satan, what can you do about it?** First you should ask the LORD to take care of the distraction. Follow His leading. It could be that He wants you to change your prayer time or location. Another possibility is that He might want you to develop a thicker skin. Sometimes we are called on to persevere and endure.

7. **Why do you think that Satan choses to interfere with your prayers?** It is part of his main function. He can be defeated. It is better to say he is defeated. Presently he is just jerking around as best as he can.

8. **Why do you think that the good LORD allows distractions?** Sometimes it is a test. He may be wanting us to call on Him. He may be allowing undesirable things to happen so that in resisting them He can build our character. If He wants you to know something, He will have no difficulty communicating it to you.

9. **Can you name the worst hindrance to prayer?** SIN!

> **"If I regard iniquity in my heart,**
> **the LORD will not hear me:"**
>
> Psalms 66:18 KJV

> **"but your iniquities have made a separation**
> **between you and your God,**
> **and your sins have hidden his face from**
> **you so that he does not hear.**
> **For your hands are defiled with blood**
> **and your fingers with iniquity;**
> **your lips have spoken lies; your tongue mutters wickedness."**
>
> Isaiah 59:2-3

> **"For if you forgive others their trespasses,**
> **your heavenly Father**
> **will also forgive you, but if you do not forgive others their**
> **trespasses, neither will your Father forgive your trespasses."**
>
> Matthew 6:14-15

10. What does "**regard iniquity in your heart**" mean? It means you have pet or favorite sins and you hold on to them and you are not sincerely asking the LORD to forgive you for committing them. Each person needs to ask the good LORD to help him or her overcome his pet sins and to become the holy person that the LORD created you to be.

11. What are some of the other verses that describe hindrances to prayer?

"Because I have called, and ye refused;
I have stretched out my hand,
and no man regarded;" "Then shall
they call upon me, but I will
not answer; they shall seek me early,
but they shall not find me:"

Proverbs 1:24 & 28 KJV

"Because they hated knowledge and did
not choose the fear of the LORD,
would have none of my counsel and despised
all my reproof, therefore they
shall eat the fruit of their way, and have
their fill of their own devices."

Proverbs 1:29-31

"If one turns away his ear from hearing the
law, even his prayer is an abomination."

Proverbs 28:9

"When you spread out your hands, I will hide my
eyes from you; even though you make many prayers,
I will not listen; your hands are full of blood.

Isaiah 1:15

"There is no one who calls upon your name, who rouses
himself to take hold of you; for
you have hidden your face from us, and have
made us melt in the hand of our iniquities."

Isaiah 64:7

"As I called, and they would not hear, so they cried, and
I would not hear, says the LORD of host,"

Zechariah 7:13

"And I will surely hide my face in that day
because of all the evil that they have done,
because they have turned to other gods."

Deuteronomy 31:18

When someone cries out to you and you choose not to pay attention
to them the LORD will do the same to you especially if you have
been disregarding His written Word.

"But let him ask in faith, with no doubting, for the one
who doubts is like a wave of the sea that is driven and
tossed by the wind. For that person must not suppose
that he will receive anything from the LORD; he is
a double-minded man, unstable in all his ways."

James 1:6-7

"You ask and do not receive, because you ask
wrongly, to spend it on your passions."

James 4:3

"When you spread out your hands, I will hide my
eyes from you; even though you make many prayers,
I will not listen; your hands are full of blood. Wash
yourselves; make yourselves clean; remove the evil of
your deeds from before my eyes; cease to do evil, learn
to do good; seek justice, correct oppression; bring justice
to the fatherless and plead the widow's cause."

Isaiah 1: 15-17

"Then they will cry out to the LORD, but he will not
answer them; he will hid his face from them at that
time, because they have made their deeds evil."

Micah 3:4

12. Can the content of our prayers be hindrances to them being
answered?

"You ask and do not receive, because you ask wrongly,
to spend it on your passions."

James 4:3

13. **What do you think the likely result of your prayers will be, if you pray and don't really expect anything to happen?** You will probably get tired of praying. You will likely begin to doubt the LORD. Your faith, if you had any, will likely dissolve into thin air.

14. **If you were to pray and had an awareness of one of your sins and you didn't sincerely ask the Father to forgive you, what do you think would result from your prayer?** If in fact you are a believer, the Holy Spirit would step up the conviction that you have sinned and need to repent. Eventually, you should expect the LORD to do something that will get your full attention. (Normally, these things are very unpleasant!) If you continue to rebel, your heart will become calloused and you will backslide until you respond correctly to a severe correction.

15. **When someone else is praying a very good prayer do you join them in prayer in your spirit? Why?** If you pray with them, what do you think it indicates. If you don't, what does that indicate?

16. **When you hear someone pray for a worthwhile need, do you ever discern that their prayer words were just that a bunch of nice sounding words, how do you react in your spirit?** I should pray for them and ask the LORD what He would have me to do. It could be His will for you to pray for them!

17. **When your dog, cat or other pet is having serious problems have you ever prayed for them? How about someone else's pet?** YES. Most people love their pets. Seeing God work to help them, will help increase one's faith.

18. **What type of prayers are the most difficult ones for you to pray?** Asking for His help when I am told to ask another person for their forgiveness. Asking for His will to be done when I suspect that it is something that I don't want to do.

19. **What kind of prayers are the easiest for you to pray? When you pray these prayers does your seriousness level decrease or increase? Why?** A thank you prayer. If so, then why do so many people scarcely pray them?

20. **When someone else prays out loud do you pay careful attention to what they are saying? If not why?** When we sense that they are praying about something that is Spirit led, we should join them in our spirit and also pray with them. When we don't add our prayers to theirs we are probably spiritually anemic. And probably need a massive transfusion of the Word

Verse	_Chapter_	_Page_	_Topic_
Deuteronomy 31:18	12	53	God doesn't hear.
Psalms 66:18 KJV	12	51	Sin stops prayer.
Proverbs 1:24 & 28 KJV	12	52	When God doesn't answer.
Proverbs 1:29-31KJV	12	52	When God doesn't answer.
Proverbs 28:9	12	52	Not listening to God's law.
Isaiah 1:15	12	52	Murder cuts off prayer.
Isaiah 1:15-17	12	54	God doesn't listen.
Isaiah 59:2-3	12	51	Sin separates
Isaiah 64:7	12	52	Hiding your face from God
Micah 3:4	12	54	God doesn't answer
Zechariah 7:13	12	53	God doesn't hear.
Matthew 6:14-15	12	51	Why you are not forgiven!
Matthew 6:14-15	12	53	Why you are not forgiven!
Matthew 7:7b KJV	12	55	Seek and find
Hebrews 11:6 KJV	12	54	Faith is necessary.
James 1:6-7	12	53	Don't waver in your faith.
James 4:3	12	53	Asking Him wrongly
I Peter 3:7KJV	12	55	Husband s prayer obligations

CHAPTER 13

HOW OFTEN SHOULD
WE PRAY? – PART 1

HOW OFTEN SHOULD
WE PRAY? – PART 2

1. **In a typical day, how many prayers do you think that the average believer prays?** *(In a round-about way what the person says is average could likely be the number of prayers that he prays.)*

2. **What do you consider the optimum number of prayers for the average believer to pray during an ordinary day?** ONE! But it can have many topics, pauses and should last all day.

3. **What does the scripture say about how often a true believer should pray?**

    "Pray without ceasing," I Thessalonians 5:17 KJV

4. **Often times when a believer prays there is a topic or thyme in their prayer. Is there anything more important than the topic or need that you are praying about?** YES! It is having fellowship with the Father! Why is this so important? It is one of the reasons that we were created.

> **"Abide in me, and I in you. As the branch cannot bear fruit by itself, unless it abides in the vine, neither can you. unless you abide in me."**
>
> John 15:4

5. **Is prayer the only earthly means that a believer has to fellowship with the Almighty? If not how else can a believer fellowship with Him?** When a believer is physically and or mentally doing something that the Father wants him to do and is doing it with the constant support of the Master, He is also fellowshipping with Him.

6. **How can you be in pray all day long and be in a never-ending mode?** Don't you have other things that are also necessary?

7. **How much of your prayer time should you be meditating on God's Word and the task that He has set before each of us?** Enough to absorb the thoughts that the Spirit is sending. When you have meditated enough you should wait until the Spirit changes the subject. (NOTE this may go on for a very long time for people who don't want to accept what the Spirit is communicating!)

Verse	Chapter	Page	Topic
I Chronicles 16:11	13	57	Seek the Lord continuously.
Luke 21:36KJV	13	57	Pray all the time.
I Thessalonians 5:17	13	57	Pray without ceasing.

8. **If you are trying to be constantly in prayer with the Master, what could be the cause for a break in this prayer?** Satan will occasionally try to interrupt a prayer, if he can, in order to distract you from what the Spirit is saying to you. It is also appropriate to ask the good LORD to overpower the distractions of the evil one.

9. **Does God ever disconnect a believer's continuous prayer? If so, what do you think could be the reason for this?** A disconnect is most likely when we are rebelling against the instructions in His Word. NOTE: Our rebellion is our disconnect.

10. **When our continuous prayer link with the master is broken, how can we get it back?** We can pray and ask the Father to forgive us. This should be followed with serious Bible reading on the topic that applies to our specific sin problems.

11. **Is meditation an important component in Christian prayer?** YES! **What other kinds of prayer are there?**

12. **How can you determine if a thought that is coming into you head is from the Holy Spirit?** First, you need to be in the right frame of mind. By this I mean that you have cleansed your heart by prayerfully asking the Good LORD to forgive you of your sins. Next, you should be fully willing to do God's will. The second step often requires that you have read the Word sufficiently to be aware of more of the things that the LORD wants, does, and asks. Then, you determine if the message is in alignment with Scripture. Does a verse come to mind that clearly defines and confirms what you think is the action that the LORD wants you to take? If so, you are on solid ground, if you obey Him. NOTE: The Holy Spirit and the Word work together! What can you do if you haven't read the Word? **Read it!**

13. **When you read from the Holy Bible, that you should meditate on what it is saying? Is meditation different from thinking seriously?** Meditating is an essential part of prayer. It is a link between asking the Father a question and hearing and understanding His answer. NOTE: Some thoughts take time in order for them to sink in!

14. **Can meditation of a Scripture verse be considered part of a prayer?** It is an important part. Communication consists of sending and receiving messages. Unfortunately, too many believers are just into the sending mode. His answers are more important than our earth-bound comments.

15. **If our prayer link gets broken can, how can we ever get it back?** By offering a serious "please forgive me of my sin's prayer". Pray until you are reconnected.

16. **What are some of the more common things that someone you know might ask you to pray for?** *(Note the people who do not respond to this question. Do they have a serious need that they are too shy to mention? Are they truly a believer? Are they wanting*

to give others the floor so that they can become more involved in the conversation? There are lots of possibilities. Some are good and some are not.) For too many people the people that are normally around them are not aware that they are a believer!

17. **When should you pray out loud for a person who just asked you to pray for their need?** When the Holy Spirit places this in your heart. Most of the time it is evident that they are under a heavy burden spiritually. Most of the time their need is urgent and serious.

18. **When someone's valid need comes into your mind (a need that you do not have the capacity to meet) how should you react to it?** You Pray!

19. **What prayer can you always pray in someone else's behalf?** For God's will to be done?

1. **Discuss the kinds of prayer that a good believer may offer on behalf of a stranger who is a very dangerous driver?**
   You can always pray for someone's salvation and that they would become the person of God that they were created to be.

2. **What are some of the things that you believe that you shouldn't pray for?** For harm to come to someone especially if they have done something bad that affects you. You can always pray that they will surrender to the pleas of the Holy Spirit.

3. **What are some of their needs that you should pray about?**
   Start with the spiritual and pray toward their physical needs.

4. **When you are going for a walk or are all alone does the words of a Christian song or Hymn come to mind?** When it does and you sing it either out loud or in your spirit, are you praying? When you mean and believe what you are singing, it can be a prayer.

Verse	_Chapter_	_Page_	_Topic_
Hebrews 11:6a	14	59	Faith is imperative.

CHAPTER 15

WHEN SHOULD WE PRAY?

1. **What do you think the term "praying without ceasing" means?** It includes being ever aware that the good LORD is always present with a believer. It also means that in your mind you should be either listening to Him or constantly expressing a prayer to Him. Are you on the alert for His incoming messages?

2. **How does the Holy Spirit move you to pray?** When you are in the right frame of mind for prayer, He highlights the need sufficiently. The closer you are to Him the clearer His communications are. He makes the believer aware of the many spiritual needs that you have and the needs of others. The Spirit may even lead to you pray for a stranger on the other side of the world.

3. **What should a believer do or be doing so that he or she is more sensitive to the Holy Spirit's communications to him or her?** Confessing His Sins and asking the good LORD to forgive him. Reading and memorizing the Word! Listening to Godly leaders who teach and preach the Word. **<u>OBEYING THE LORD! (Obeying has both obligations and benefits)</u>** In a few words, we need to be as holy as we can be.

4. **What should you do or be doing so that you are ready to pray or listen to the Holy Spirit within a second's notice? Is this currently possible for you?** You can begin by keeping your forgiveness prayers up-to-date. You should also be putting forth a constant effort to hear Him. Every believer should be regularly storing Scriptures in their mind.

5. **How do you define the term "First Aid Prayer"?** A prayer need is suddenly presented to you. It can be from another person or your spirit may be quickened to pray immediately for a need. NOTE 1: This is not a replacement for the extended daily prayer appointment that you have with the good LORD. NOTE 2: The prayer need can be in an area that is outside of your gifting. Even when you do not have the Spiritual gift that would best serve the situation, any believer can always pray for a person or situation and the ability to help as the Holy Spirit leads him.

6. **What time of day do you think is best for your extended time of prayer? How flexible should we be when we schedule a prayer time?** Many believers get up early so that they can begin their day with prayer. Others wait until there is a lull in their work that allows them adequate time to pray. Some wait until bedtime in order to be able to pray extended prayers without being distracted by daily events. Some may have more than one scheduled prayer time. If in doubt, ask the good LORD to guide you.

7. **What kind of place do you believe is best for prayer? NOTE: In some European castles the owner had a chapel built just for prayer? What does this type of prayer closet indicate to you?** Sometimes when I am traveling or at work the best place I can pray in in a bathroom. The LORD provides. Our job is to follow His directions. He will provide what is needed. It may not be our choice but it will be sufficient.

8. **Would any one care to tell the group about a time where the Holy Spirit moved him or her to pray a specific prayer for something or someone without any earthly knowledge about the reason or need? Let us now pray silently for the person that comes to mind. Would any one care to share some of this prayer?**

9. **If I were to ask each of you to bow your head and pray silently for someone you know and haven't communicated with for a long time or have any current knowledge about their needs, could you do so? Let each of us now bow our heads and pray silently for someone from our childhood, or whomever the LORD puts in our mind.**

10. **How does belonging to a believing congregation help you with your prayer life?** You will have the examples of good heart felt prayers. You will be exposed to more of God's Word. You will have the privilege to pray for the needs of more people.

11. **Praying is communication with the Almighty. Communication should always be a two-way street. Normally, you say what you need to say to the Father; then, you listen and await His response. Why don't believers listen to the Father first and then pray for our concerns? Is there anything that you can do to improve the listening part of your prayers?** Yes, near the top of the list should be meaningful Bible study, every day! When you do this you will be more alert to what the Spirit says to you through the Word and His responses will be much clearer.

12. **How do you become aware of something that the good LORD wants you to do?** You nurture the seeds of thought that the Holy Spirit plants in your heart. This is supercharged when you are prayerfully reading the Word and meditating on it.

13. **Are there things that you can do to improve your spiritual hearing ability?** Yes. Pray sincere forgiveness prayers. Sin less and increase your serious Bible study. What else can you do? The more you choose to follow the Spirits leading the clearer His instructions will be. Be Holy!

14. **Are there things that you should avoid in order to hear the LORD easier and clearer? What are the distractions that are the hardest to avoid?** Worldliness! It is part of human nature to want to blend in with those around you. Each of the people you choose to associate with will have an effect on your lifestyle and spiritual condition. Hopefully, you will have a godly effect on them.

15. **What do you think could be God's criteria when he selects someone to pray for another person?** That the person's prayers would be helpful to the person that needs them, that they are under the control of the Holy Spirit, and that the one Who is praying could also get a boost to his or her faith.

16. **Does prayer seem to consume spiritual energy? If you think it doesn't, then have you considered why**? Are you praying like the Father would have you to pray? Are you just saying a bunch of words with no spiritual value?

17. **How do you get more spiritual energy? Can you use it all up?** Through prayer, Bible study and practicing what the Holy Bible instructs you to do. It might be hard to scientifically prove but I think it is possible to get considerable spiritual energy and strength from others who are praying for you.

18. **Is there a benefit to having an accountability partner?** Definitely. It can either be a formal regular meeting to discuss the spiritual aspects of your life and behaviors or it can be a more casual conversation. Let the Good LORD decide what you need and be obedient to Him. It could be that you are the first person to ask them to be your spiritual accountability partner and they are the one who needs the experience. Everyone hast to start somewhere!

19. **How do you get an accountability partner? What should you look for when considering someone for this task?** Make efforts to form friendships with people who you believe are more spiritual than you are and let the Holy Spirit lead you.

20. **Have you ever considered becoming an accountability partner for one of your friends?** Why would they want you for this responsibility? Could it be that the people that you have chosen to associate with are not good believers? Ask yourself this Question. What reasons could they give for not wanting to be spiritually accountable to you?

21. **What are some of the practical considerations that should affect the time you select for your special prayers with the Father?** A quieter time of the day, a time when you can be alone, a time when there are the fewest distractions. A time where the length of your prayers is not limited or boxed in between other activities. (For those who are planning their prayer time, for their first time, 30-45 minutes is a reasonable starting point.)

Verse	_Chapter_	_Page_	_Topic_
I Thessalonians 5:17KJV	15	61	Pray without ceasing.

CHAPTER 16

WHAT SHOULD WE NOT PRAY FOR?

1. **Are there things that you shouldn't pray for?** If they are sinfully oriented or things that are definitely out of God's will, don't pray for them. You should pray for deliverance from evil temptations and for forgiveness. The spiritual downfall of anyone is a good specific example of a do not pray topic.

2. **What is the strangest thing that you ever prayed for and your prayer was clearly answered?** (If the answer was NO! is still an answered prayer.)

3. **You prayed for something and nothing happened. Does that mean that the answer was NO?** Not necessarily. His answer could be, "later". It could be that you need to pray for the good LORD to open your eyes so that you can see His answer. Both yes and no answers should be clear. If not, it is OK to pray for more clarity. Sometimes it might be helpful to rephrase your prayer.

4. **As a believer should you have a list of things and people that you feel that you should pray for or about regularly?** It's up to you. There are plusses and minuses either way. Why not ask the Father for directions. He will lead you in the way you should pray. Trust Him! **(You may have noticed by now that many of my thoughts are basically simple. Life is relatively simple. Sin complicates everything around it!)**

5. **What is the most convincing proof that you have that the good LORD loves you?** He hasn't zapped me on the spot when I so often deserved it.

6. **How should you complete a prayer where you ask the Father for something that you dearly want?** You ask Him to override your request, if it is outside of His will.

7. **Did Jesus ever ask the Father for something that He dearly wanted? When?** In the Garden of Gethsemane. see Matthew 26: 39-44 **What happened?**

8. **When someone has done something grievously wrong to us should we pray for God to punish them?** The sad truth for some of us is that God is not slack when it comes to punishments. He is also a God of love. The scriptures say to love your enemies!

"**But I say unto you, Love your enemies, bless them that curse you, do good to them that hate you, and pray for them which despitefully use you, and persecute you;**"
                                                                    Matthew 5:44 KJV

Also see: Matthew 5:43-48, Romans 12:20, Luke 6:27, Leviticus 19:18, Romans 12:14, Luke 23:34, and 1 John 4:7 **When the same thought is expressed this many times in Scripture it is very important.**

9. **We should know not to pray for any selfish passions. What other passions or unholy matters should we include on the list of do not pray prayers?** Prayers based on: Greed, lust, pride sinful desires, It is a very long list!

10. **Can an act of prayer, due to its content, become a sin?** Yes! It could also be a sin to omit praying for some spiritually good things. NOTE: NONE OF US ARE SPECIAL EXCEPTIONS!

11. **When is it a sin to not pray?** When the Spirit leads you to pray and you decide not to. It can also become a sin to pray for something that you believe is out of God's will. Always let your prayers be Spirit led!

12. **When should a believer decline the opportunity to pray publicly?** When he has unconfessed sins that he needs to fully confess. He should decline when the Spirit leads Him to not pray. It could be that the Good LORD wants someone else to pray the public prayer. If we are spiritually out of kilter and are not willing to begin our prayer by asking for forgiveness, we are not ready to pray about anything else. What is our present spiritual condition? How do we get out of this condition? We always have choices. We can either sincerely pray for forgiveness or we can wait until the LORD decides that enough is enough and He takes appropriate corrective actions. The grief and pain are not worth the temporary pleasure of sin.

13. **When we sense that God's answer is NO! And we still feel compelled to keep on asking for something that we want, what should we do?** If the request was a holy request and Scriptures clearly approve of the actions, then it could be that the LORD wants you to do things both physical and spiritual that would support others who are doing this work. Another

possibility is that He wants you to wait and become better equipped to do the task. God knows best, thrust Him! Seeking His will is always the best thing to do. At times it can be a very difficult thing to do!

14. **When we are asked to pray publicly and we want to impress others with our praying ability, what sin are we committing?** PRIDE!!!!!

15. **When we are being interviewed for an advancement or a new job, what should we pray for?** That God's will is done and that we make the impression THAT WOULD Honor The Father. His will is more important than any job. If the LORD wants you there, you will be there. If you don't get the job, remember the good LORD designed you He knows what you need. He will provide!

16. **When someone has done something really bad to us or a friend what prayers should we pray?** That the wrongdoer become the man or woman of God that He created them to be. Sometimes it is God's plan for them to be converted in Jail. It has happened many times. For example, after my father retired he got a part time job as a prison chaplain. One of the inmates had had a crime filled violent life. One time when the prisoner was in solitary confinement he was given a good Christian book. He read it and for three days this hardened criminal was in tears,

repented of his sins and became a new creature. His life changed so much that he received both state and federal pardons. While he was in prison he earned a degree in Bible from a nearby Christian college. After he was released he returned to prison as a chaplain to help the other prisoners. The short answer: Forgiveness prayers!

17. **Is it necessary to name every sin that we want forgiveness for?** It would be nice if we could. But each of us has sinned so much that we would not have time to do anything else. However, it is very appropriate to ask the good LORD to bring to our mind the sins that we need to specifically confess and to tell us if there is anything else that He would have us do. It has been my experience that the LORD doesn't normally dump all of them on us at once and that this is an ongoing lifetime obligation. There is a big difference between naming a sin and making an excuse for it!

18. **Which sins should we specifically name when we are praying for forgiveness?** When the Holy Spirit convicts us of a specific sin. NOTE: His conviction is different from the reminders that Satin brings to our mind sins that we have already ask for forgiveness that we are no longer committing. **Satan always wants you to identify as a sinner. Jesus wants us to identify as a saved sinner.**

19. **Do good believers pray for things that they shouldn't pray for?** Yes! But this can be taken care of very easily. Just add this footnote to all of your request. Dear God may your will override anything that I have asked for that is outside of your will. NOTE: If you don't mean what you pray, it doesn't count in your favor!

20. **Think over the last few requests that you made to the Father. You can still ask Him to override any request that are outside of His will. He's waiting!**

Verse	_Chapter_	_Page_	_Topic_
James 4:3	16	64	Asking Him wrongly

CHAPTER 17

DESPERATE PRAYER

1. **Has anyone ever had an occasion where "desperate prayer" was the only hope that you had? Would anyone like to share that event with us?**

2. **What is a desperate prayer?** Something happens and it turns your world up-side-down. This experience supersedes everything else that you are doing or that you are planning to do. Whether it is sickness or some terrible accident, it has your full attention. Many of these are for the purpose of the good LORD getting our full attention. It might be possible to avoid some of them by constantly giving the LORD the respect that He deserves.

3. **What are some of the reasons for the desperate prayers that people pray?** Healing, escape from impending danger, for life itself. (NOTE if anyone said that praying for the salvation of a lost person was a desperate prayer. If not, mention it when the response comes to a close.) **What is more important than salvation?**

4. **Are all desperate prayers urgent?** Do they quickly become unnecessary after a short period of time? I.E. When someone is falling off of a tall building.

5. **Are some desperate situations avoidable? If so how?** By daily praying for God's will to be done and then following it the best you can. Rebellion has a high cost!

6. **What is an example of a universal desperate prayer?** "HELP"

7. **How would you define a HELP prayer?** It is what you pray when you think that you or your loved ones have only a fraction of a second of life left. Or when you have prayed so much regarding a desperate need that "Help" is all you can verbalize.

8. **What type of prayer could you pray in order to minimize a future unknown bad event where a help prayer would be necessary?** You can commit the future events to the good

LORD! You should also obey the LORD when His Spirit moves you not to do or to do something. It could be a simple thing that you do every day that in itself was not sinful.

9. **What should you be doing so that you are as ready as possible when the awful occasion requiring a desperate prayer suddenly drops on you?** 1. You should keep your forgiveness prayers as up to date as possible. 2. You should memorize the content, if not the exact words, of as many prayer promises as you can. 3. You should commit each trip or activity to the good LORD and ask for His protection and guidance.

10. **How does a person manage to keep their forgiveness prayers current and up to date?** Pray them often and include them at the beginning of every prayer.

11. **What are some of the basic prayer promises that you should learn first?**

"He shall call upon me, and I will answer him: I will be with him in trouble; I will deliver him and honour him."

Psalms 91:15KJV

"Before they call I will answer; while they
are yet speaking I will hear."

Isaiah 65:24

"And I tell you, ask, and it will be given
to you; seek, and you will find;
knock, and it will be opened to you. For
everyone who ask receives, and
the one who seeks finds, and to the one
who knocks it will be opened."

"Luke 11:9-10

"If you abide in me, and my words
abide in you, ask whatever you
wish, and it will be done for you. By this my Father is glorified,
that you bear much fruit and so prove to be my disciples."

John 15:7-8

"If my people who are called by my
name humble themselves, and
pray and seek my face and turn from
their wicked ways, then I will
hear from heaven and will forgive their
sin and heal their land."

II Chronicles 7:14

"Therefore I tell you, whatever you ask in prayer,
believe that you have received it and it will be yours."

Mark 11:24

12. **Why is it important to request the LORD's help in the smaller less complicated things that you think that you can handle alone?** 1. Your faith is increased every time you receive a positive answer to a prayer. 2. Each believer needs to cultivate his relationship with the Master! Asking for His help should not be a new experience for any believer.

13. **Some desperate situations last over a long period of time? What could you do differently in these conditions?** Pray and fast, and asking other believers to pray for the need. NOTE: If you can't or shouldn't do a traditional fast, there is always something that you enjoy that you can choose to do without in order to not be distracted when you pray.

14. **What is the one desperate situation that each of us will eventually face?** Death! Are you ready to go? A believer should be more concerned about the things that he thinks the LORD may want him to do now.

15. **What are some examples in Scripture where desperate prayer was called for and was positively answered?** Moses' prayer at the red sea, Paul in jail, Sampson chained to the building column.

16. **Why do some people wait until a desperate terrible situation occurs before they call on the LORD for forgiveness?** They probably think that they can get along without the LORD's help. The LORD has no problem getting our undivided attention!

17. **When a believer has been slack in his spiritual life what does the good LORD usually do in order to get his full attention?** Sometimes it is extreme actions. Other times He touches the heart so that the person will respond to His LOVE. He knows us better than we do. He knows what we need in order for us to get on the narrow path that he has planned for us.

18. **Can some desperate situations be avoided? Yes. How? Being obedient has its advantages.** When we need correction, He provides generously. When we choose to follow His Word there is the potential for rewards. NOTE: The best rewards are spiritual!

19. **As a believer how should you react when a friend is having a desperate situation?** We should pray for their betterment and that they end up being in God's Will.

20. **Do you react differently when the person who is having the desperate situation is a stranger? Yes!** When we know them, it is sometimes easier to pray openly for them to have both a physical and spiritual victory. When we don't know them we can always pray silently, and help them as we are led. Sometimes it is very difficult to pray for close relatives. Hopefully, we can get a spiritual foothold and be enabled to pray boldly, vocally, and help them spiritually.

Verse	_Chapter_	_Page_	_Topic_
Ezra 8:23	17	66	fasting and imploring God
(Esther 4:16)	17	70	Esther's desperate prayer
Proverbs 3:5-6KJV	17	68	Trust in the LORD.
Acts 4:31	17	66	Powerful prayer
I Corinthians 10:13	17	69	resisting temptations
James 5:16 KJV	17	69	powerful prayer

CHAPTER 18
DANGEROUS PRAYERS

CHAPTER 19

PRAYER LIST

1. **Can a prayer be dangerous?** Yes! A wrongly motivated or disrespectful prayer can bring on a severe correction. The LORD does what He needs to do in order for us to become holy.

2. **What is an example of a dangerous prayer?** When a parent asks the good LORD to do whatever is necessary in order for his children to choose to become believers, the believer is literally putting his life, health and his earthly advantages on the line. Only a godly, loving parent is can do this. Sometimes the LORD's answer is very gentile. Sometimes it is not! He does what it takes to heal a rebellious heart.

3. **What are formula prayers?** They are a feeble attempt to control the Almighty so that our will instead of His will is done? It is a prayer that the designer of the prayer believes that the good

LORD will have to answer his wishes his way. Instead of asking the Father for His will to be done. It is a miscarriage of a person truly claiming a Scriptural promise.

4. **Why are they considered dangerous?** They are an attempt to control the Almighty.

5. **Can a prayer contain all of the correct words and correctly express Scriptural approved concepts and still be rejected? If so, why?** If the words we prayed were not our honest thoughts to the Father, don't expect any positive answers. Each prayer should be 100% honest and we should mean everything that we say. If we say that we are sorry for doing something, we should mean every word of it. You can't lie to God and get away with it! He knows our innermost thoughts.

6. **When can a believer quote Scriptures to the Father?** When the believer means every word of the quoted verse. It should be a Holy Spirit lead prayer. Note: The Father is keenly aware of His Word. He wrote it!

7. **Looking back at some of your prayers, how should we examine them?** Ask yourself: Why would the Good LORD choose to help me with this? How would this request advance His kingdom? Is it possible that this request is outside of His will? Is there a Scripture verse that indicates that this could be part of one of God's special activities?

---

8. **Do any of you either have or know of people who have a prayer list? Is it a written list or is it just a mental list? Do you often add or subtract names or needs? Are the needs listed in any particular order or groupings?**

9. **Lots of people have prayer list.** Is there a Scripture that mentions or suggests the concept of having a list?

10. **What are the positive aspects of such a list?** If you have promised a lot of people that you would pray for them each day, then this is a positive way that you can keep that promise.

11. **Are there any negative aspects to having a prayer list?** One can easily get into a routine where he forgets to whom he is praying. It also can leave out the Holy Spirits part in our prayers. Prayer is not a task or duty! It is a joyful communication with the LORD.

12. **If you use a prayer list what do you need to guard against**? Just repeating words and phrases that you don't sincerely believe.

13. **Some people format their prayers and recommend their format to others. What is the problem that can be associated with using someone else's prayer format? (By saying format, I mean something like" praying for yourself first, then family, friends, neighbors, etc.)** It is easy to place format over the act of allowing the Holy Spirit to have His leading in every part of our prayers. Prayers should always be guided by the Holy Spirit! He leads we follow!

14. **What are some of the problems in using someone else's prayer format? Not every prayer need will fit one of the subheadings.** Some needs are very unique. If we are placing our wants ahead of becoming more holy, then it could be that we

are wrongly applying God's Word to our prayer needs. Always let the Holy Spirit lead in all of your prayers.

15. **After you have prayed for everything on your list, what else should you do?** You should have a friendly conversation with your Heavenly Father! You can begin by asking the Father to help you to follow **His** leadings.

16. **After you have said everything that you feel that you need to say, what should you do next?** Read the Word and Listen! Then pray some more. The most important part of our prayers is listening to the thoughts from the LORD.

17. **What is the most important feature in a believer's prayer?** He must be praying in the Spirit.

18. **How does a believer pray in the Spirit?**

    "Likewise, the Spirit helps us in our weakness. For we do not know what to pray for as we ought, but the Spirit himself intercedes for us with groanings too

deep for words. And he who searches hearts knows
what is the mind of the Spirit, because the Spirit
intercedes for the saints according to the will of God."

Romans 8:26-27

19. **Given the spiritual approach to events that demand desperate prayers. Can you apply any of these verses to lessor events?** Bible principals apply to every detail of life. Just because we might think something is of lessor importance to us doesn't mean that it is less important to the Father.

20. **Do you think that your life could be better if you applied these Spiritual guidelines to more of life's events?** There is a huge difference between quoting a verse, thinking that it is a good verse and correctly applying it to your life under the direction of the Holy Spirit.

Verse	_Chapter_	_Page_	_Topic_
Romans 8:26-27	19	75	Functions of the Holy Spirit

CHAPTER 20

ASKING OTHERS TO PRAY
FOR YOUR NEEDS

1. **How does a believer decide which prayer needs to share and which needs he shouldn't?** First it should be about a serious matter. The most important thing that you need to do is to ask the good LORD to guide you and to help you to make the right decision and to follow the path that is in His will.

2. **How do you decide which people to share your prayer needs with?** The first step is to recognize that additional prayer is needed. The second step, once you decide to share a request is to make a list of believers in whom you have prayer confidence. This is where being a member of a local church comes in handy. Many times, there are people who have a need to know i.e., your pastor and the elders and deacons of your church. Some of these are your friends and relatives. Ask yourself one basic question before sending anyone your notice. Can these people keep a confidence and not use it as a seed for gossip? Next, ask the Holy Spirit to guide you in sending out the request and to guide you in what to say and how to say it. (Normally, I ask each person, may I put them on my prayer request list. So far no one has turned me down.)

3. **By what means do you use to share your prayer requests?** You may need to use various means. Not everyone uses the internet. I prefer to use email because I can send e-mails to just the people that I can trust.

4. **What are some of the dangers associated with sharing confidential needs with some people?** They may be prone toward gossip. Some may forward it to someone that you cannot trust.

5. **What is the best way of sharing prayer requests over the internet?** I prefer an email with only the address' (BCC) of the ones I trust and select to be on it. Personally, I don't trust any web site. I store the names and e-mail addresses in a Word document. That way I only need to copy and paste. If needed, it is easy to add or subtract names.

6. **What do many churches do to help believers share their prayer requests?** Many churches have prayer list. Some are on websites others are on paper. Some are oral. Many require that that you ask for prayer. If in doubt ask your pastor.

7. **What is the most important consideration one should choose when sharing prayer requests?** Are you following the leading of the Holy Spirit?

8. **What should a believer do if he hast to travel away from home? He still has prayer needs!** He can always devote more personal time to prayer. He can often communicate back home. Sometimes the best thing is to have friends who will be praying for you. When it is possible you should associate with a believing church where you are temporarily located.

9. **Why should a believer carry a paper list of names, addresses, phone numbers and email addresses of others that he can trust and count on for prayer needs?** His cell phone may be stolen or the battery might give out. A paper list can also be used by a stranger in case you are not physically able to communicate. It is sometimes very useful for another member of your family to have access to a copy of this list. If you live alone you might consider giving a copy to your pastor or to a good friend.

10. **How do many churches facilitate prayer requests?** They have prayer meetings, many of them are on Wednesday nights. If you are away from home check with a church in the vicinity that you are in.

11. **The Bible instructs believers to confess their sins.** When should this be done privately and when should it be done publicly? The rule-of-thumb that I have heard for a long time is to confess publicly, sins that were committed publicly and confess privately, sins that were committed privately.

12. **Is it best to share prayer request fully or in stages as things develop?** You can do both. Always follow the leading of the Holy Spirit!

13. **What should be the underlying thyme of all prayer requests?** *"May God's will be done!"* **Why?** There is nothing better!

14. **What are some of the benefits of having others pray for your needs?** Some people are more righteous than you are. It could be that the good LORD wants to bless them by letting them see their prayers answered for you. Answered prayer builds faith!

15. **Should weaker believers be included in your prayer requests or should you focus only on strong believers?** Selecting people to pray for your special needs should always be a matter of prayer. Let the Spirit move you. Weaker believers also need to have their faith boosted.

16. **Should you include friends, who are not believers when you send out prayer request? Why?** You can, but be careful that you don't give them the impression that you consider them to be believers when you know that they aren't. Perhaps a seed of faith can be planted where it is needed.

17. **Who may benefit if my prayers are answered?** Answered prayers can benefit not only the people who prayed for you but the people that they tell about how God answered their prayers.

18. **What is the best benefit of an answered prayer?** Faith is increased!

19. **Why does the Father want us to pray to Him?** It is the closest fellowship that we can have with the Father, while we are still alive on planet earth! Having fellowship with the Father is one of the main reasons we were created.

20. **Do non-believers have prayer needs and how can we respond to them?** They have many. They are, however, not able to properly communicate with the good LORD. This is where you can help out. You can always pray for them. If the Holy Spirit leads, you can explain the always answered prayers. i.e., Please forgive me. May God's will be done, may the LORD guide me so that I can bring the most glory to His name, etc.

HOW SHOULD A BELIEVER RESPOND TO PRAYER REQUEST

IMPERATIVE PRAYER OBLIGATIONS

1. **Why do people make prayer requests?** Many people realize that the LORD can do anything and that some people are better able to pray effective prayers than others. Scriptures tell us to bear each other's burdens. Prayer is one of the ways we can do this.

> **"Bear ye one another's burdens, and so fulfil the law of Christ."**
>
> Galatians 6:2 KJV

2. **How should a Believer respond to a prayer request?** He should pray that the LORD's will is done! Oftentimes, there is something else that you can and should do. Ask the good LORD to guide you.

3. **When should a prayer be silent, prayed out loud or prayed later at the believer's regular extended prayer time?** Some prayers, by their very nature, should be prayed privately. Others, by their nature, should be bold, oral, and public. Some believers experience a closer relationship with the Father when they pray their private prayers orally. You can never go wrong by praying as the Spirit leads you.

4. **How do you know how to respond to another person's prayer need?** You quickly pray a silent prayer asking God to forgive you of your sins; then, you specifically ask the Holy Spirit to lead you in the way that He wants you to proceed!

5. **How should a believer pray when he personally wants something?** He should pray for it and close the prayer with a clear statement that if the thing he is praying for is outside of God's will, that He would override the request.

6. **How should a believer respond to a news broadcast interview where the person being interviewed request prayer?** Believers should respond to all request for prayer. Your prayer is your

prayer and should always be for someone's betterment. Always pray that God's will is done. There is nothing better!

7. **How should you as a believer respond when an out of the blue a stranger almost causes an automobile accident with you being the victim?** You should thank the good LORD for protecting you. Secondly, you should pray for the spiritual benefit of the other driver. He obviously needs much prayer. It is also good to pray for both of you to become safer drivers.

8. **What prayers are believers obligated to pray?** For the salvation of the lost. For their leaders and pastors. For God's will to be done. There may be few prayers that a believer is obligated <u>NOT</u> to pray. **What do you think some of them are?**

9. **What are the requirements for a need to become an imperative prayer obligation?** When it becomes serious enough that. if the believer doesn't pray about it. that it becomes a sin of omission.

10. **What is the prayer need that each believer has that is often overlooked?** Fellowship with the Father. It is one of the reasons that were created. NOTE: It is a lot more than just thanking and praising Him.

11. **What is the surest way a believer can meet all of his prayer obligations?** By constantly obeying and joyfully following the leadership of the Holy Spirit!

12. **Can a good believer do the LORD's work all by Himself?** No! Everything must be done under the leading and help of the Holy Spirit. Note: Even the simple things that anyone thinks that they could do by himself are done much better when they are done under His leadership.

13. **Who is a believer obligated to pray for?** Everyone who request his prayers and everyone and everything that the Holy Spirit urges him to pray about?

14. **How should a believer react when someone that they don't know does something or says something that indicates that He or she is lost?** He should pray that they will come to believe in Jesus and ask Him to forgive them of their sins. When you become aware that a person is lost it is an indication that the LORD might have an assignment for you that could lead toward their salvation.

15. **Who else that the believer doesn't know or is only able to name should a believer pray for?** He should pray for to lots of people: Policemen, mayors, senators, other representatives' various bureaucrats, the flight crew on a plane that he or his friends and associates are traveling on. The list is endless. See I Timothy 2:1-2

    "First of all, then, I urge that supplications, prayers, intercessions, and thanksgivings be made for all in high positions, that we may lead a peaceful and quite life, godly and dignified in every way."

16. **Choices and selections are a part of everyone's life.** Any time we are faced with a choice, a believer should ask the Holy Spirit to guide him into making the decision that the good LORD would have him make. Some of these are very obvious and others are seemingly neutral. **What are some of the recent choices that you made and how did you make them? Were**

they obvious, neutral or somewhere in between? Rightly or wrongly, we tend to make many choices automatically without any thought or prayer!

17. **What should a believer expect if he doesn't do what the good LORD created him to do?** Sufficient motivation to do God's will! A correction! NOTE: just because the correction is not always instantly done doesn't mean that the good LORD is slack. It could be that He is allowing you a generous amount of time to repent before He acts. He takes no joy in punishing or correcting His children. People who are not one of His children don't receive these corrections. This thought should be troubling to someone who is living a sinful life and thinking that he is a believer. See **Hebrews 12: 5-8**

18. **What one thought should every believer include with ever prayer request?** That the LORD's will is done.

19. **Why is that so important?** There is nothing more important than Gods Will!

20. **When should a believer not pray for something that he wants**? When the Holy Spirit has tells Him that it is outside of God's will. Many times, this is done through the Holy Bible. When you choose not to read it and give it the priority that it deserves, you are resisting the Holy Spirit and God's will!

Verse	*Chapter*	*Page*	*Topic*
I Timothy 2: 1-4	22	94	Pray for those in authority.

CHAPTER 23

BECOMING EQUIPPED TO BE HOLY

1. **Is it likely or even possible for any human being to become 100% holy on this side of Heaven?** NO! **Then what is realistic for a good believer?** To become much holier than he or she currently is!

2. **How is this done?** To a degree each believer, who is up to date in his forgiveness prayers and Bible readings/**STUDIES,** is at lease moving toward becoming holier. The more submissive a believer is to the Holy Spirit the holier he becomes. Holiness like any other spiritual quality starts with prayer and is followed up regularly with more prayer and acts of submission to the urgings of the Holy Spirit. It is not a do it yourself project! Holiness is an ongoing series of heart felt holy choices. Choosing to do God's will!

3. **Something to think about. Why do so many distractions seem to happen when you decide to pray or study the Bible?** Could it be Satan's attempt to interfere with your spiritual growth? Do you get sleepy? Does the phone ring? Does someone knock on your front door? Do you remember that your favorite TV program is about to start?

4. **There are non-believers who have read the Bible several times and can cite verses on many topics but they are not holy nor do they desire to become holy. What are the differences between the way they read the Bible and the way a good believer should read the same Bible?** (Note the people who tend to think that it is the same!) One only gains information, the other builds his faith and receives guidance.

5. **What is the biggest difference in the attitude of a casual reader of the Word and a true believer who reads the Word? What are the two competing attitudes?** The believer reads his Bible as part of his communication to the Savior, who died a miserable death and rose again so that he might be saved. It is a detailed "letter" from his very best friend. The other reads it as an attempt to figure out how God decides who to reward or as a matter of pride. Selfishness does not bring happiness! **As a believer have you ever read your Bible with the wrong attitude? Can you name one person who hasn't?**

6. **When you start reading the Bible do you pray about it? What should be included in this prayer?** 1. You should ask the Father to forgive you of your sins. 2. You should ask the Father to minimize any distractions that might come your way. 3. You should ask the Holy Spirit to open your eyes and guide you.

7. **What are some of the "spiritual tools" that are mentioned in Ephesians 6: 11-19? How are they acquired?** Via prayer and Bible study!

8. **What happens when someone who is holy sins?** Ideally, he will seek repentance quickly because of the strong urgings of the Holy Spirit to repent and to seek God's and everyone else's forgiveness. **NOTE: This is a vital part of spiritual warfare!**

9. **How should they follow up these prayers?** By sincerely asking for the Holy Spirit to help them to lead a more Holy life.

10. In Ephesians chapter six the first tool that is mentioned is **the belt of truth. How would you describe this tool and why do you think it was mentioned first?** A person's faith is essential to living the Christian life. If a person has doubts about the truth of God's Word, he will fail until these doubts are replaced with true Biblical belief.

11. The next tool mentioned is the **breastplate of righteousness. How would you describe this tool and why is it essential?** You can't expect the Good LORD to protect you from the attacks of Satan unless you are obeying the Holy Spirit by being the person that the LORD designed you to be. The LORD expects each of us to conduct ourselves in a holy manner.

12. **Why do these verses include shoes for your feet?** They can remove us from danger and when we are led by the Holy Spirit, and they can carry a person through perilous places where the Gospel needs to be proclaimed.

13. **What is the readiness given by the gospel of peace? What is the gospel of peace?** See: **Philippians 4:7, Galatians 5:22, Isaiah 26:3, John 14:27, and John 16:33.**

14. **What is the function of the shield of faith?** To stop the fiery darts of Satan from harming us. Satan will at every opportunity cast doubts in our path. Faith in God and in His Word deflect these doubts.

15. **What is the purpose of the <u>helmet of salvation</u>?** It protects our most vital organ. When the head goes, life is gone. The helmet of salvation represents the fact that once a person is truly saved he is saved forever.

16. **Why do you think Paul compared the spiritual tools of a believer with the equipment that the Roman army used in his day?** Everyone had seen Roman solders and knew that they were the best army in the known world at that time. He was emphasizing the fact that believers too were in a spiritual conflict and that they too are provided with excellent equipment. It is only a matter of putting it on and using it under the leadership of the Holy Spirit! He used the things that they knew about to explain truths that they needed to understand.

17. **Are there any other Spiritual tools that a believer has and should use regularly?** The communication tool of PRAYER! **Why do you think Paul didn't mention prayer in this list of spiritual tools?** The Roman army did not have walkie-talkies!

18. **Are there any other Spiritual tools that today's believers have access to?** The complete and very available Holy Bible, the Church and the spiritual gifts that the LORD gives each believer.

19. **What are some of the battles that believers have and how should we use these spiritual tools today?** Temptations are all around us. We default to temptations every time we try to fight a battle with our home-made do-it-yourself weapons.

20. **What is the difference between the spiritual battles that they had verses the ones that we have today?** In many cases their battle included many terrible physical consequences. Today's battles normally result in believers giving in to lite social pressures.

Verse	*Chapter*	*Page*	*Topic*
Ephesians 6:11-19	23	96	the whole armor of God
(Ephesians 6:14)	23	97	the belt of truth
(Ephesians 6:14)	23	98	the breastplate of righteousness
(Ephesians 6:15)	23	98	shoes for the feet
(Ephesians 6:15)	23	98	Gospel of peace
(Ephesians 6:16)	23	99	shield of faith
(Ephesians 6:17)	23	99	helmet of salvation
(Ephesians 6:17)	23	99	the sword of the spirit

HOW DO YOU THANK THE ALMIGHTY? - PART 1

HOW DO YOU THANK THE ALMIGHTY – PART 2

1. **How do you say, "Thank You" to the Almighty? Better yet, why should you thank God for what you are grateful for?** Unfortunately, too many "believers" are not appreciative or thankful for the many wonderful gifts that the Father has so generously given them. Saying "thank you" is a lot more than pronouncing the words. True thankfulness comes from a sincerely grateful heart for the blessings that were received. Many of these are spiritual and some of them may be physical. **How much do you value your blessings?** Being thankful is more than just acknowledging the receipt of them. It includes joyfully using them to honor one's Savior. NOTE: Some believers are thankful about the things that God has said that He will do in the future and for bad things that didn't happen.

2. **Does the LORD expect us to thank Him for all that he is doing for us?** Being thankful includes using His various gifts for the purpose that He gave them to us. In all likely hood, when

we are thankful we are demonstrating not only our appreciation but we are acknowledging the fact of the LORD's supremacy.

3. **Is a sincerely spoken "thank you" sufficient?** Never! Not even for gifts that others give us. Believers should strive to use His gifts for the purpose that the good LORD had when He gave them to us. Normally, this is done by prayerfully reading His Word and obedience.

4. **What should every believer thank Him for?** Salvation and an ongoing relationship with God. What else? The Holy Spirit. The list never ends. Have you ever thanked Him for the privilege of fellowshipping with Him? Since this is something that a believer can choose to have as often as he pleases, then why don't we do it more often. Do we think something else is more satisfying or more important?

5. **How sincere are our thank you prayers to the good LORD?** Not sincere enough! We all have human limitations. Blaming our shortcomings on our humanity will not suffice. He knows what we are capable of doing and being.

6. **What about the good things that we have ignored?** Even good believers tend to take most of the good things and good relationships for granted. Should we lose them, we will begin to understand some of their worth. When He sees that removing some of them will help us grow spiritually, He can easily remove them!

7. **What about the bad things that could have easily come our way and didn't? How should we express thanks?** When we look at the problems that people around us are having, it is easy to see many things that the good LORD has spared us from experiencing. The close calls where another driver came very close to hitting us. A person we know got mugged on the same street that we walk on. Things that could have happened and didn't are one of the biggest gaps in our thanksgiving prayers!

8. **Why do you think the good LORD gives us the things that He does?** He truly loves us! Many if not all of these blessings were given to us for His good purpose. Believers should use them in His will. When we don't know His will for something that He has given us, we should ask.

9. **Is it humanly possible for any person to properly thank the good LORD for anything that He has chosen to do for him?** NO!

Verse	_Chapter_	_Page_	_Topic_
John 14:15	24	103	Love produces obedience.
Philemon 1:4	24	102	Thank God for other believers.

10. **What are some of the gifts that most believers overlook when they are thanking the good LORD?** One of the often-overlooked things that we should be thankful for is the good testimony and godly activities of other believers. This is illustrated in the Book of Philemon.

> **"I thank my God always when I remember**
> **you in my prayers, because I hear of**
> **your love and of the faith that you have toward**
> **the LORD Jesus and all the saints,"**
>
> Philemon 1:4

11. **What is a major problem with many thank you prayers?** Semi-enlightened self-interest. We do things that we think will please Him because we believe that He will do more good things for us. This is not an expression of thanksgiving. It is a feeble

attempt to entice the creator of the universe into doing more good things for us. He knows what motivates us better than we do.

12. **What are some of the ways of properly showing the Father that we are thankful for His many blessings?** The best way a believer can respond to God's love is to purpose in his heart for God's love to flow through him to others.

13. **The question is how does the average believer know what is an honest heart felt praise and what is not? Or can he?** The average believer can't even know his own heart much less make truthful spiritual judgements concerning others.

> **"The heart is deceitful above all things, and desperately wicked: who can know it?"**
> Jeremiah 17:9 KJV

14. **How can a true believer express his thanks to the Father?** Praise is one way a believer can honestly express his thanks to the LORD.

> **"But you are a chosen race, a royal priesthood, a holy nation, a people for his own possession, that**

you may proclaim the excellences of him who called
you out of darkness into his marvelous light"

I Peter 2:9

15. **Why is praise so important?** One of the purposes of praise is to inform others about our wonderful LORD! This should be an extension of sincere thankfulness. A satisfied customer is still the best advertisement for anything!

16. **What would you consider a defective praise?** One where the one doing the praise did not mean the words they were saying. Another variation of this is when a person goes through the motions and words of praise only for the purpose of gaining favor with the Almighty.

> **"The heart is deceitful above all things,**
> **and desperately wicked: who**
> **can know it. I the LORD search the**
> **heart, I try the reins, even to give**
> **every man according to his ways, and**
> **according to the fruit of his doings."**
>
> Jeremiah 17:9-10 KJV

17. **What are some of the ways that a believer can express praise to the Father?** In the spoken word, in song and in Holy Spirit led actions.

    "Rejoice in the LORD, O ye righteous: for praise is comely for the upright. Praise the LORD with harp: sing unto him with the psaltery and an instrument of ten strings. Sing unto him a new song; play skillfully with a loud noise."
    Psalms 33:1-3 KJV

18. **What did the author think was the highest form of worship that a believer could have on earth?** Praise!

19. **Can you name some songs that express praise to the Father?**

20. **Can you name a hymn that <u>doesn't</u> express some aspect of praise to the Father?**

BEING ALONE WITH THE FATHER

FAMILY PRAYERS

1. **What are some of the things that you think most people are reluctant to pray about?** Their personal pet sins, for God to save or help the people that they don't like, etc.

2. **What are the three modes of prayer?** Speaking to the LORD, listening to what He has to say and meditating on His Word.

3. **What do you suspect happens if you leave any of the components out?** Considerably less!

4. **Does a prayer end when you have said and done each element?** NO! Prayer should always be an ongoing spiritual activity.

5. **How long should a prayer be?** As long as you need in order to ask everything you need to ask and to say everything that you need to say and the hear everything that you need to hear? There are no time requirements but it should not be considered unusual for a beginner to pray 15 to 20 minutes. A devout believer will normally pray much longer!

6. **What can you do to improve your spiritual hearing ability?** You can be reading your Bible under the direction of God's Holy Spirit! And following its instructions as best you can.

7. **What are the various factors that you should consider when you select a time for your special extended prayers with the Master?** Select the times when you are least distracted by other things? It is good to pray in the mornings and ask for the LORD to guide you through-out the day. Forgiveness prayers are best as soon as you realize that you have sinned. Thank you prayers are good at the end of the day. **PRAY WHENEVER AND HOWEVER THE SPIRIT MOVES YOU TO PRAY!**

8. **By what means does the LORD normally use to communicate with you?** The Holy Spirit! This is best done while you are seriously reading the Word!

9. **Some people quote a Scripture verse when they are asking the Father to do something?** What are the pluses and minus of doing this? Remember the Scriptures are for our benefit! The LORD wrote them. He doesn't need our reminders. Some people misuse Scriptures by trying to use them like a club to beat Him and anyone else that they disagree with into compliance. Think before you quote, **am I speaking from my new nature or from my old nature!**

10. **What can you expect every time you pray?** Distractions?

11. **Where do distractions come from?** Many come directly from Satan. Some are due to our own carelessness. What can you do to minimize them? Some people turn their phone off. You can select a better time to pray your longer prayers. Some distractions are predictable. Work around them as best you can. The best thing you can do is to ask the good LORD to help you so that you and Him can meet and be undistracted!

12. **When you want something is there any reason why you shouldn't ask the Father for it?** If it is not sinful or wrongly motivated you should ask. **BUT** always add one condition "that if it is outside of God's will that he would keep it from you". When you feel that you can't add this you are the one with a serious problem!

13. **What thought should accompany every request?** "Thy will be done". It is always appropriate to thank Him for exercising His will.

14. **When you are praying and ideas flashed through your mind is it always God speaking to you?** NO! Test the spirits! Compare the thoughts with the Holy Scriptures! Where in the Bible does it mention _____? This is one of the many reasons why you should be reading your Bible every day. It is also a good reason for owning a Thompson Chain Reference Bible and a complete concordance. With these tools you can usually find the answer quickly. You can also use Duckduckgo.com and type in where in the Bible does it mention _____. Even if you don't have any of these you can still get your answer. Many times, you can ask a pastor or someone you know who is in a positive relationship with the good LORD and get your answer. Don't expect effortless answers!

---

15. **How often should a family pray together?** Once a day is good. Whenever there is an urgent serious need, pray!

16. **What concerns should a parent have when there are small children present?** Age-appropriate topics! You can always pray about other topics when you are alone or with your spouse. Even when it is about someone committing the worst of sins, you can always pray for the good LORD to guide them to a condition of holiness.

17. **What is a good way of starting Family prayer times?** By reading a Bible story. Egermeier's Bible Story Book" is excellent. It's available on eBay.

18. **How should a very young child be encouraged to pray?** First by example. You can ask them to pray with you a simple prayer. As they get a grasp of prayer they should be encouraged to pray with you and on their own.

19. **Should different members of the family read scriptures or should it be the same parent every time?** Make sure that each person has the opportunity to participate in family prayer many times. A shy child might need to be asked some simple questions so that they are drawn into the devotion time. Help them as best you can, everyone is different but we all have a need for the Savior!

20. **If the family pet is having problems is it appropriate to include them in your prayers?** Yes! If the pet gets well you should thank the good LORD. If he doesn't you can remind everyone that it was his time to go. Answered prayer builds faith. Should the pet die it is an opportunity to explain that sometime in the future each of us will also pass on. For the believer this is our trip to be with the LORD.

21. **What options can you exercise if one member of the family hast to be away at prayer time?** Email and phone prayers work. If this is not possible, the parent that is present can remember the other parent in prayer. In single parent homes it may be necessary to have an older child occasionally read the scripture and pray for the family. You might consider a list of scriptures and prayer request for them to use as a guide. If a sitter is with them ask them to read the verses for them and if they are a

believer then you might ask them to pray. If not, ask them to call on an older child to pray. It may have a very good effect on them! Do the best that you can.

22. Does family prayer replace individual prayer? NO!

CHAPTER 28
PUBLIC PRAYERS

CHAPTER 29
PRONOUNCEMENTS

1. **Why should there be a prayer at a meeting where secular items are to be discussed?** Even in secular matters the good LORD has interests that are appropriate. In some cases, He will bless the ongoings and in others He may choose to move people into a better direction. He may even make the meeting very efficient so that you can finish early and go on to a spiritual assignment.

2. **What criteria should be considered when asking someone to open a meeting with prayer?** Their relationship with the Master.

3. **What is a poor reason for starting a meeting with prayer?** To get everyone to be quiet. Some devious people may want to open with a prayer that would try to convince those who are ignorant of God's Word that an evil activity is really OK!

4. **If you are called on to pray at a public meeting what are the things that you should consider before answering?** Am I up-to-date in my confession of sins? Does the LORD want me to pray? What does the LORD want me to say, if anything, in the group's hearing?

5. **Is there a topic in the meeting that has spiritual components? Can you name a concern that doesn't have a spiritual element attached to it?**

6. **Are some meeting topics inappropriate to pray for?** Definitely! Many popular causes are contrary to God's Word!

7. **If you are going to pray publicly what should you do beforehand?** Pray silently and ask the Father for forgiveness and to give you the words that He wants you to speak.

8. **What kind of prayer needs a human audience?** A prophetic prayer.

> "For the LORD does nothing without revealing
> his secret to his servants the prophets."
>
> Amos 3:7

9. **Can you give an example from the Bible of public prayer?** Solomon's prayer dedicating the Temple is recorded in **I Kings 8:22-54**.

10. **How should you react when the person who ask you to pray puts restrictions on what you can say?** If you are asked to pray contrary to Scripture, just decline.

11. **When someone prays publicly, what do you expect the LORD to do as a result of that prayer?** Bless the activities of the meeting. NOTE; Some activities are not blessable.

Verse	_Chapter_	_Page_	_Topic_
Amos 3:7	28	114	The LORD informs His prophets
Acts 1:14	28	113	Being in one accord
Acts 12:12	28	113	Group prayer

12. **What is a pronouncement?** It can be a type of short prayer where the one saying it is stating what he is convenienced the LORD would have him to say. Normally, this is a request for the LORD to do something supernatural.

13. **What are the various types of pronouncements mentioned in Scripture?** Blessings and curses, and prophetic utterances are the main ones.

14. **Why are pronouncements included in a book on prayer?** The aim of the pronouncement is usually beyond the ability of the person doing the pronouncement. He is in effect praying for the LORD to act in a particular situation.

15. **Can pronouncements be a type of prayer?** Definitely!

16. **When is a blessing statement a prayer and when is it just another social thing that people say?** When the intent is that the good LORD blesses someone. It is a prayer to the Father

asking Him to do something special for them. Otherwise, it could be just another polite statement. For example, someone sneezes and you say "bless you".

17. **What is the difference between a virtuous statement and a spiritual pronouncement?** A virtuous statement is manmade. (NOTE: Just because it is manmade, it is not automatically worthless.) A spiritual pronouncement by a believer who is following the leadership of the Holy Spirit is a statement that the LORD wants voiced. It is a most serious statement. One should be extra sure before making such a statement. **How would you categorize a statement where someone rebukes Satan?**

18. **Why should a person be extremely careful about using their presumed spiritual power of attorney attaching Jesus 'name as a co-signer to any pronouncements?** There can be grave consequences for distorting or lying about what the LORD wants said!

19. **Can you as a believer pronounce a curse on an enterprise? If so under what circumstances is this acceptable?** Yes! But it should only be done only under the guidance of the Holy Spirit! In one sense it could be a statement of support for the Scripture that says:

"Vengeance is mine saith the LORD"
Romans 12:19b

20. **Why should a believer never tell another person to go to the place of never ending punishment"?** The LORD GOD ALMIGHTY is the only one with that authority. You never want to be in the position of usurping His authority!

21. **What are the components of a curse? How close to a curse can you get before you have gone too far?** Hoping that Bad things happen to someone is going too far. Praying for the LORD to correct a bad condition is appropriate.

Verse	_Chapter_	_Page_	_Topic_
Jude 1:9	29	116	Rebuking Satan

CHAPTER 30

SPECIAL PURPOSE PRAYERS – VOWS

1. **What is a vow? Is it any different from a promise?** A vow is a very serious promise made officially to the LORD. When you make a vow, you are communicating to the Father. Communication with Him is PRAYER! The one saying it correctly is not only promising to do or to not to do something but to put forth every possible effort that he can in order to keep the vow. It can also indicate that the person making the vow desires the LORD's help in keeping the vow. A promise from an honest person should be regarded the same way; however, in practice many people attach unspoken stipulations that they think will allow them **not** to do the thing that they said they would do. **Many people that claim to be honest or even think that they are honest, aren't!**

2. **What are some of the different types of vows?** One of the most common vows is the wedding vow. In Old Testament times the Nazarite vow was taken by some.

3. **How do you think the LORD reacts when a believer breaks a sacred vow?** Sternly! He doesn't always choose to act quickly but He always reacts appropriately.

4. **If a person keeps a vow in spite of difficulties, what can he expect the good LORD to do?** Recognize the effort. Some people mistakenly think that they should be rewarded for every little thing that they do. His rewards are valuable and are determined by His wisdom. **Our personal desire for a reward doesn't help us in any positive way. Seeking His will always has very good possibilities.**

5. **What are covenants? What is the difference between a vow and a covenant?** There are two kinds of covenants. The Biblical type is where the, for His own reasons the LORD makes an offer to do something. Usually, there is a condition that the object of the covenant does something that the LORD requires. Men often break their agreements and the LORD always does exactly what He said that He would do. The Second type is actually a misuse of the Biblical term. Today the word is used in some cases in place of saying a legal agreement. Vows and covenants are very serious promises.

6. **What does the Bible say about swearing an oath? Don't swear! See** (Matthew 5:33-37). **What does the law in the United States say in regard to swearing an oath i.e., in court?** You can affirm that you are speaking the truth. In the early days of American many people believed that if you swore an oath and

lied that you would go to never ending punishment. Hence, in courts of law witnesses are required to swear an oath in order to get to the truth.

7. **Can you identify a vow that Jesus may have made?** He could have been a Nazarite. Scripture is not 100% clear on this. He did do things that were consistent with this vow. This is not to be confused with the fact that He was from the town of Nazareth.

8. **Can you identify others mentioned in the Bible who made a vow?** (Acts 18:18)

9. **Exactly what was included in the Nazarite vow. See** (Numbers 6:2-21)

10. **How many covenants does the Bible mention?** 1. The Edenic, Genesis 1:26-3:24 2. The Adamic, Genesis 3. The Noahic, Genesis 8:21. 4. The Abrahamic, Genesis 13:14-18. 5. The Mosaic, Exodus 19, and John 19:30, also called the Palestinian

covenant) 6. The new covenant, Hebrews 8:8-13. 7. The everlasting covenant, Genesis 17:13. 8. The Davidic covenant, II Samuel 7:8-16, Psalms 89, Psalm 110 and Danial 2:44.

11. **What should you expect if you broke a promise?** To be considered unreliable at a minimum. In many cases a liar. Lying can have extreme consequences!

12. **What does Scripture say about lying and liars?**

"…and all liars, shall have their part in the lake which burneth with fire and brimstone: which is the second death."
Revelation 21:8bKJV

13. **What should a believer do if the Holy Spirit convicts someone of lying, breaking a promise, breaking a vow, or breaking a covenant?** He should sincerely repent and ask the good LORD and any one that he lied to, to forgive him. It is then his job to earn back their trust by being humble and honest in every way.

14. **Is a person lying, if he is literally speaking the truth but has carefully crafted his words so that the truth is camouflaged?** Instead of just being a liar he has become a deceitful person who should not be trusted. This is a very bad condition to be in!

15. **Is there a spiritual difference between lying and being deceptive?** Both are so bad that it would be useless to distinguish between them.

16. **If you are asked to tell someone something and afterward you find out it was false how should you react?** You have a high obligation to correct it as soon as you determine that what you were told to say was false.

17. **What are some of the vows that people make today?** A wedding vow. Unfortunately, many people don't even try to keep it! Others have decided just to "live in sin".

18. **Under what conditions should a person refrain from making a vow?** When they have a reason to believe that they cannot keep it!

19. **How should a believer react if someone made a vow to you and you later found out that they broke it?** If they ask for forgiveness you should forgive them. NOTE: Unlike the LORD, you will remember it and will tend to watch them carefully.

20. **Are there conditions and circumstances where it is acceptable to break a vow or a promise?** When it is impossible to keep? This is rarely true. If you find yourself in this condition the best thing you can do is to ask them to release you from the vow. You have made a very serious mistake!

Verse	_Chapter_	_Page_	_Topic_
(Numbers 6:2-21)	30	119	A Nazarite vow
Ecclesiastes 5:5	30	119	better
(Matthew 5:33-37KJV)	30	117	Don't swear.
(Matthew 5:37KJV)	30	118	don't swear.
Revelation 21:8bKJV	30	118	Lier's fate

BLESSINGS

CURSES

1. **What is a blessing? A true blessing is when the LORD does something beneficial for you.** It can be something that someone else or yourself has requested or it can be something that the good LORD chose to do independently. A blessing is usually done for a purpose. Many times, people are blessed and they are not aware of it. In all cases we should thank the good LORD for each of them.

2. **Can you give an example of a blessing that is in the Bible?** Genesis 32:29, Luke 1:28

3. **Why do many believers say a blessing before eating a meal?** Unfortunately, too many people do it just as a matter of habit. The blessing before a meal should always include a thank you prayer!

4. **Some people tend to say the same words when they are saying a blessing before a meal. What caution should they be aware of?** Memorizing the blessing and praying it without thinking about what you are saying. All prayers should be sincere and heart felt. Just reciting a bunch of religious words is disrespectful to the Almighty. If you always pray the same words you can easily slip into not communicating with the Father.

5. **What should a person expect to happen when they casually say, God bless you," to someone?** In most cases NOTHING! When it is said as a sincere prayer, true blessings should be expected.

6. **The Bible mentions examples of a father pronounced a blessing on one of his children. Is this an appropriate thing to do today?** YES!

7. **Can you give examples of blessing that were pronounced or received by someone mentioned in Scripture?**

    Isaac blesses Jacob **Genesis 27:26-30.**

    **"And if you will walk in my ways, keeping my
    statutes and my commandments, as your father
    David walked, then I will lengthen your days."**

    I Kings 3:14

The book of Ruth contains a wonderful blessing:

**"The LORD repay you for what you have
done, and a full reward be given you by
the LORD, the God of Israel, under whose
wings you have come to take refuge!"**

Ruth 2:12

8. **Can a believer receive a blessing without asking for it? Yes!
But how much appreciation does the average believer have for
these blessings?** Unfortunately, when something good happens
too many people, including some believers, consider themselves
lucky. The word lucky comes from the word Lucifer, which
is another name for Satan. One should not expect anything
good to happen by associating something good that came from
the good LORD by implying that it came from Satan. i.e. a
correction.

9. **When you decide to ask the Father to bless someone or
something, what precautions should you take?** Be careful
that in the process of making pronouncements that you don't
carelessly bless an activity or purpose that the good LORD has
disapproved.

10. **What are some of the causes, activities, etc. That are in society today that shouldn't be blessed?**

11. **What are some causes or activities that you think that the LORD would like you to bless?**

12. **How am I supposed to know what the LORD approves and disapproves?** You study the Holy Bible! If in doubt, you can always pray and ask The Holy Spirit to guide you. The Holy Spirit doesn't contradict the Word.

13. **How should a believer react when he becomes aware that the good LORD has given him a blessing?** Humble and thankful. He should then ask the Father how he wants him to use the blessing that he has received. Blessings have a Devine purpose.

Verse	_Chapter_	_Page_	_Topic_
Genesis 48	31	121	family blessings
(I Kings ch. 3)	31	120	Solomon's conversation with the LORD

NOTE: In some cases, it may be wise to skip the part of this lesson it deals with* "curses" especially if someone in the group tends to jump to a conclusion or has demonstrated a bad temper. EXERCISE GOOD JUDGEMENT AND WISDOM!

14. **What is a curse?** A curse is a type of prayer where the person pronouncing it is in effect asking the good LORD to punish someone or something.

15. **Who can pronounce a curse?** Anyone! Who can pronounce an effective curse? A Believer who is acting under the direction of the Holy Spirit. There are cases where nonbelievers have pronounced effective curses. (Where do you think they got the power to pronounce effective curses?) I believe that their curses are more effective when they are pronounced against nonbelievers.

16. **Why do people pronounce a curse?** Many times, it is an effort to get revenge.

> "Dearly beloved, avenge not yourselves, but rather give place unto wrath: for it is written, Vengeance is mine; I will repay, saith the LORD."
>
> Romans 12:19

(NOTE if vengeance is appropriate, The LORD can do a much better job of it than we can.)

17. **What do you think might be adequate reasons to justify a curse?** Justifying a curse is a very difficult thing for any human to do correctly!

18. **What happens if a curse was not justified?** One of the consequences of pronouncing an undeserved curse is that it may backfire and the curse could land on the one who wrongly pronounced it.

> "Like a sparrow in its flitting, like a swallow in its flying, a curse that is causeless does not alight."
>
> Proverbs 26:2

19. **If you are considering pronouncing a curse, what should you do first?** Tread carefully. Curses should be exceptionally rare and one should seriously pray about the matter before pronouncing them. Like a blessing the one pronouncing them is in effect attempting to say something that the good LORD wants said. This is an enormous responsibility and is not to be entered into lightly. If you can't find a Scripture that supports the curse, then you will probably be better off by not pronouncing it.

20. **Why are curses included in a book on the topic of prayer?** A curse is a spiritual pronouncement. It is in effect a type of prayer that request the LORD punish someone or something for being severely out of line with God's Word and hindering or menacing His will being done.

21. **What does the Bible say about curses?**

    Here are a few of the many verses that mention curses.

    "I will bless those who bless you, and him who dishonors you I will curse, and in you all families of the earth shall be blessed."
    Genesis 12:3

    "You shall not revile God, nor curse a ruler of your people."
    Exodus 22:28

"You shall not curse the deaf or put a stumbling block before the blind, but you shall fear your God: I am the LORD."

Leviticus 19:14

"How can I curse whom God has not cursed? How can I denounce whom the LORD has not denounced?"

Numbers 23:8

"See, I am setting before you today a blessing and a curse: The blessing, if you obey the commandments of the LORD Your God, Which I command you today, and the curse, if you do not obey the commandments of the LORD your God, but turn aside from the way that I am commanding you today, to go after other gods that you have not known."

Deuteronomy 11:26-28

"bless those who curse you, pray for those who abuse you."

Luke 6:28

"Bless those who persecute you; bless and do not curse them."

Romans 12:14

22. **Does a curse have to have the word "curse" in it in order for it to be a curse?** See Nehemiah 4:4-5. Here a curse was pronounced in a prayer to punish the people who were seriously hindering God's will from being done.

23. **Did you sense a feeling of empowerment when you read the chapter on curses?** If so. you should examine your standing with the good LORD. The Holy Spirit will guide you but the decision is always up to you.

Verse	*Chapter*	*Page*	*Topic*
Genesis 12:3	32	124	Blessings and curses
Exodus 22:28	32	124	Don't curse a ruler.
Leviticus 19:14	32	124	Don't curse the deaf.
Numbers 23:8	32	124	Only curse those God curses.
Deuteronomy 11:26-28	32	124	Curses and blessings
(Nehemiah 4:4-5)	32	125	Nehemiah's curse
Proverbs 26:2	32	123	Underserved curses
Luke 6:28	32	125	Pray for abusers.
(Acts 13:6-12)	32	125	Peter curses a sorcerer
Romans 12:14	32	125	Curse not.

CHAPTER 33

INTERCESSORY PRAYERS

1. **What is intercessory prayer?** It is a prayer where a believer sincerely asks the good LORD to help someone else.

2. **Who is qualified to pray an effective intercessory prayer for another person?** Any believer who is up-to-date in asking the good LORD for the forgiveness of his own sins.

3. **Who is definitely unqualified?** Active sinners! (Everyone who hasn't ask Jesus to save them!)

4. **Does the Father ever answer the intercessory prayer that is made by an unbeliever?** He can do anything that He pleases. However, it is unlikely that an unbeliever can persuade the good LORD to do anything unless he first sincerely asks the LORD to forgive him of his sins. In that case he is no longer an unbeliever.

5. **What prayer should a believer pray first before praying for someone else?**

What can you do if you are the only believer in a situation and you don't have any means of contacting someone who is more righteous to pray for a desperate need? You pray the most sincerely honest repentance prayer that you can and ask the Father to make you righteous and then you pray for the desperate need. NOTE: The good LORD will instantly know if you really meant your prayer. You may not! If you honestly repented of your sins and ask the Father to forgive you and you fully intend to live a righteous life the Father will react to your prayer for His will to be done! He may do much more than you expect Him to do.

Scriptures tell us that:

> **"The effectual fervent prayer of a**
> **righteous man availeth much."**
>
> James 5:16b KJV

6. **Under what circumstances do you think that the good LORD would want you to ask others to pray for a special need?** When He wants to use His answer to favorably affect the ones that prayed for you. NOTE: A few believers can rightfully be classified as prayer warriors. It is their spiritual assignment from the LORD! It can be considered a special gift and a special calling.

7. Scriptures tell us to **"Bear one another's burdens and so fulfill the law of Christ."** Galatians 6:2 Intercessory prayer is one of the ways believers can do this. **How else can this be done?**

8. **What is the likely result of God answering a prayer?** Everyone who prayed for the need will have their faith strengthened.

9. **How do you know who to pray for?** God's Holy Spirit will motivate you to pray for the needs of others whether or not they have requested prayer.

10. **What might happen if you are moved to pray for someone's need and for whatever reason you don't pray?** The other person may have his answer delayed or cancelled. His burdens may even increase.

11. **What are some examples of intercessory prayers in the Scriptures?** III John 1:2, Acts chapter 12

12. **What should I ask the Father for when I am praying?** Don't worry about how the good LORD is going to work things out. Just trust Him to do the things that he has already chosen to do. His response is far better than anything that we can imagine. NOTE: Don't fall into the trap of telling the Almighty, all Knowing Creator of the Universe how He needs to help out in a given situation. Just ask Him to do the best thing that He can. He is a lot smarter and many times more powerful than we can imagine. Trust Him! He loves each of us very much!

13. **Are their people with whom we strongly disagree and that we would consider earth a better place if they were gone? Are we expected to pray for any of them?** Definitely!

> **"First of all, then, I urge that supplications, prayers, intercessions, and thanksgivings be made for all people, <u>for kings and all who are in high positions, that we may lead a peaceful and quite life, godly and dignified in every way.</u>"**
>
> I Timothy 1-2

14. **What are some of the reasons why intercession is necessary other than faith building?** There are conditions where the LORD has chosen not to hear an individual's prayer. Yet, He may be willing to respond to a more righteous person's prayer. For example: Job 43:8.

15. **What is the main condition where the LORD has already decided not to hear a specific person's prayer?** Unconfessed sin!

16. **What elements are most likely present in a righteous person's prayers that is praying for your need?** For personal forgiveness and for God's will to done.

17. **What is a negative possibility of having a very large number of people pray for your need verses having a small select number pray for you?** The Large number could easily include a lot of backslidden Christians who falsely believe that they can gang up on the good LORD and cause Him to follow their wishes!

18. **How many of you can recall an event in your life where a group of believers successfully interceded for someone who needed prayer?** Would anyone care to share the experience?

19. **Has anyone ever made an agreement to fast and pray, with another believer, for the spiritual betterment of a third believer?** Would anyone care to share the experience?

20. **When a believer feels that he needs prayer and does not request it, what do you think the reasons are? Where did these feelings come from?** An inactive prayer life tends to be a habit for some people. Others may be afraid of what they think the good LORD may be asking them to do. These feelings always come from Satan.

Verse	_Chapter_	_Page_	_Topic_
(Job 42:7-9)	33	127	Job's intercessory prayer
(Acts 12)	33	129	Peter gets out of jail.
Galatians 6:2	33	127	Bearing other's burdens
Ephesians 6:18	33	126	Effectual prayer availeth.
I Timothy 2:1&2	33	126	intercessory prayer
James 5:16bKJV	33	126	Confession of sins
James 5:16bKJV	33	127	Confession of sins
III John 1-2	33	129	Intercessory blessings.

COMMITMENT PRAYERS

PRAYERS FOR GUIDANCE

1. **What is a commitment prayer?** A commitment prayer is a prayer that a believer prays concerning a future event. In it the believer expresses his trust in the Almighty to take care of a problem and its outcome so that His will is done. It also expresses confidence in the love that the Almighty has for the believer. It is an act of trust, submission, obedience, and most of all love.

2. **On what occasions are commitment prayers necessary?** Any occasion that the Spirit moves the believer to think that there is a problem or that future problems may occur. This is especially necessary when a person's faith is going to be tested. Are there events that do not, in some way, test one's faith?

3. **Name some Scriptures that encourage commitment prayers?**

   **"Commit thy way unto the LORD; trust also
   in him: and He shall bring it to pass."**
   Psalms 37:5KJV

> "Commit thy works unto the LORD, and
> thy thoughts shall be established."
>
> Proverbs 16:3KJV

4. **What is an example of a commitment prayer that is in the Bible?** A better question could be to name a prayer in the Bible that is not is some way a commitment prayer.

5. **Why are commitment prayers so powerful?** They are a form of praying for God's will to be done. A prayer that is always answered in the affirmative!

6. **What is a common mistake that many well-meaning believers make when they pray?** They try to tell the Almighty, all Knowledgeable God how to do his job in a specific matter!

7. **What does praying a commitment prayer demonstrate?** 1. That you trust the Almighty. 2. That you believe that The Almighty is also all knowing. 3. You know that the Almighty truly loves you.

8. **When the good LORD takes care of a problem that you committed to Him what should you do?** 1. Thank Him! 2. Commit other concerns to His good judgement. God apparently likes to demonstrate to His people that He truly loves them.

9. **Why don't more believers pray commitment prayers?** 1. They don't trust the LORD. 2. They think that they know what he will choose to do and their old sin nature desires something different! 3. They are ignorant of what the Word says.

10. **What are the positive results of a believer praying a sincere commitment prayer?** 1. The LORD intervenes and causes better things to happen. 2. The believer's faith is increased. 3. Sometimes non-believers are awe struck at what the LORD does. Sometimes they become believers.

Verse	Chapter	Page	Topic
Psalms 37:5 KJV	34	134	Commit your way.
Proverbs 16:3KJV	34	134	Commit your work.
Matthew 26:41	34	133	Watch and pray

11. **What is the difference between a commitment prayer and a prayer for guidance?** Commitment prayers are much broader in scope. They include all things related to the problem that was committed to the good LORD. Whereas prayers for guidance usually deal with making choices and asking for directions. As a practical observation it doesn't matter how we classify a prayer. Either way we are trusting the good LORD for a good outcome.

12. The LORD gave each of us a brain. **Why can't we just use the brain that he gave us?** Our brain is corrupted by our old sin nature. He knows the outcome of every choice that we could make. At our best, we can only make a good guess. There is always some facet of a problem that we don't completely understand.

13. **Can you give some examples of someone in the Bible getting directions from God?** Gideon (Judges 6:25: 25-27), Paul, (Acts 10: 10-15)

14. **What condition should you be in before requesting guidance or praying a commitment prayer?** You should first ask the good LORD for forgiveness and then ask that his will is done.

15. **What should you do if you prayed for the good LORD's help and as best you can determined nothing happened?** EXERCISE PATIENCE!

    Next, you should determine if your prayer got through to the master? This is a matter of spiritual trouble shooting. First, you need to seriously determine if you are harboring any sin in your life. Next, you should Ask the Father to forgive you of your sins and to bring to mind any sins that you specifically need to deal with. When you have allowed God's Spirit full control of your life you can then re-pray about the item that you need help with. You should also ask Him to give you the patience that you obviously need in order to abide in Christ while you are waiting for His answer.

16. **What should I be doing while I am waiting on the LORD to help me with my problem?** You should be deeply involved in purposeful Bible study that relates to the problem. NOTE: Serious Bible study is a lot more than just reading a few extra verses. It is a dedicated effort toward finding God's will.

17. **What else should I be doing?**

> **"In all thy ways acknowledge him, and
> he shall direct thy paths."**
>
> Proverbs 3:6 KJV

18. **What is the most important aspect of both commitment prayers and prayers for His guidance?** Having faith that His will is done!

19. **What is the one thing that the Good LORD wants for all believers.** That they strive for holiness!

20. **Can anyone become holy?** Yes! Anyone can but they must first become a believer. On earth holiness is a never ending effort. In heaven it is automatic.

Verse	*Chapter*	*Page*	*Topic*
Proverbs 3:6 KJV	35	137	God directs your paths.

CHAPTER 36

HOW DO I RECEIVE HIS ANSWER?

1. **How many of you have ever prayed and asked the good LORD for His help?** *Note: some people that don't answer or raise their hands may be shy. Others who raised their hands may have been dishonest. Don't make judgements on others!*

2. **How many of you have gotten a clear answer from the LORD and you are confident that it is His answer to your prayer?** Ask if anyone would like to share?

3. **Has the LORD ever given you directions without you asking Him for them?** Ask if anyone would like to share? **Better yet, why haven't we noticed the directions that He is constantly giving us?**

4. **Why do you think the LORD wants the believer to ask for directions before He gives them to the believer?** He wants the believer to know where His answer and help are coming from. It is very easy to slip into pride and try to take personal credit for a good outcome!

5. **What is spiritual discernment?** The ability to understand something that the Holy Spirit is wanting to communicate to you clearly enough for you to make the decision or take the action that you are presented with.

6. **Why is it so difficult to decern a clear answer from the LORD who loves each of us so much?** We are all sinners and have a sin nature. Yes, even good believers have a sin nature. Believers also have a new nature! Which one do you allow to control you? **Which one do you feed the most?**

7. **What are God's official (preferred) communication links that He uses to communicate with us?** The Holy Spirit and the Holy Bible.

8. **Does He ever use additional communication methods?** Yes! All the time.

9. **So, what does a believer need to do in order to properly use these communication assets?** Keep up to date in his forgiveness prayers! Study the Bible daily and pray for God's will to be done. Then he should also be putting forth a sincere effort to become more sensitive to the murmurings of the Holy Spirit.

10. **How does a person do this?** By using the Spiritual power that the Good LORD gave you to resist the temptations of the Devil. Every time a believer resists a temptation to sin he grows spiritually.

11. **How does a believer know if the answer he is getting is the one that the LORD sent him or is it a counterfeit answer sent from Satan?** By reading the Word and by listening to the Holy Spirit. Even then, some things must be spiritually discerned over a period of time.

12. **What are some of the false signals that Satan sends to believers?** Satan will often try to distract a believer with all sorts of temptations. Some may be Scripturally OK but they are not what the good LORD wants you to do now.

13. **Counterfeit signals are common. In order to be a counterfeit, it needs to have at least the appearance of having some truth.** Can anyone give an example of a counterfeit signal that contains at least a small amount of truth? A believer may be choosing between two very good Scriptural assignment possibilities. He asks for Gods will to be done. A third possibility arises and the believer is now confident that it is the LORD's will.

14. **How can you determine if a signal is a false signal?** By comparing it with God's Word and by listening to the Holy Spirit and asking the LORD for guidance. Sometimes, He may choose to give you a confirmation.

15. **How quick does the good LORD answer?** He is not in a hurry. He answers when the time is right. Not sooner, not later.

NOTE WELL! Sometimes He chooses to use another human being to convey some thought to you. If He does, what criteria do you believe that He has in choosing who to use? 1. Is this a very important Spiritual decision that the LORD strongly wants you to make? 2. Sometimes He assigns a message to a person that He is training to do something special. 3. Has the Holy Spirit ever used you to convey a thought to another person?

16. What did God promise in His Word to believers?

"Ask, and it will be given, to you, seek and you will find; knock, and it will be opened to you. For everyone who asks receives, and the one who seeks finds, and to the one who knocks it will be opened."
Matthew 7:7-8

17. How does a believer search through the Bible and find the relevant Scriptures concerning the answer that relates to his problem? There are many ways. Basically, one reads the Bible until the Holy Spirit highlights the verse that he or she needs. This can be very time consuming. This is why each believer should be reading the Bible every day. Over a period of time, he will become familiar with the Word and will either know what it says or will have a fair idea about where he can find his answer. Another way is to use the concordance that many Bibles have in the back section and do a key word search. One step better is to use a complete concordance that covers every word in the Bible. Another positive and many times quicker step is to use a Thompson Chain Reference Bible and look up the key words in the index. The Index will refer the reader to a number. The number section is just after the index. For major topics all of the main verses are printed out. The minor topics have just the reference verses that the reader will need to look up individually. Many times, I have googled a question: What does the Bible say about _____? So far, I have gotten a good answer each time.

One can also ask his pastor, elder, deacon, Sunday School teacher about the topic. In emergencies you can always pray a "HELP!" prayer. (What we think is an emergency and what He considers an emergency may be different!) There are many ways of finding Scriptural answers to our many problems. You can always rely on God's Holy Spirit! NOTE: He places a high value on being patient!

18. **What does our "free will" have do with receiving answers from the good LORD?** The free will aspect begins when we decide which of our two natures we are going to feed. Whatever is nourished the most tends to flourish, grow, and influence us. By the time the matter matures most of the decision to do or not to do an action is essentially made. Often times the LORD's answer is just wait until I am ready to tell you.

19. **What can I do if I don't get an answer?** Sometimes for various reasons the good LORD will want you to wait for His answer. It is not what we want but it is exactly what our loving Heavenly Father knows is best for us.

20. **What should I be doing while I am waiting for His answer?** You should be nourishing your new nature and starving your old sin nature. NOTE: The LORD has many things that He wants each of us to do. His schedule is often different from ours.

21. **Sometimes His answer comes in bits and pieces. What should I do then?** Start obeying each one as He gives it to you in best way that you can.

Verse	Chapter	Page	Topic
(Judges 6:36-40)	36	141	Confirming God's will
(II Samuel 7:18-29)	36	141	David ask God to confirm his prayer.
Matthew 7:7-8KJV	36	140	God directs your paths.

CHAPTER 37

BUT IT IS NOT THE ANSWER I WANTED

PRAYERS FOR FORGIVENESS

1. **A devout believer can sincerely pray for a good thing. He can even find Scriptures that seem to support the prayers that he is praying, yet the good LORD may see things differently. He may choose not to answer the believer's prayer his way. How can this be consistent with all of the other teachings about prayer?** The good thing that we are praying for now may be part of a more complex plan that the LORD has for the future. To answer now could interfere with a far better action that He has planned. NOTE: Even very devout believers don't have 100% perfect knowledge of the Word. (Don't run ahead of Him and don't run behind Him. Just walk with Him! His will is always perfect.) Just abide in Him!

2. **What should I do now?** First, you can search the Scriptures and determine if the answer or lack of an answer is consistent with Scripture. If you find that your request is inconsistent with the Word, then you are the one who needs to change. You can ask the LORD to show you what you presently need to know and do.

3. **What should I do with an answer that I don't like?** Embrace it. You can always ask the good LORD to help you understand what you need to understand. Ask yourself, why do you think the LORD answered the way He did?

4. **How should I react to an answer that I don't like?** First, examine it and see if it might lead you toward something better. Ask yourself if His answer could be part of a process to make you a better Christian. The odds favor Him wanting each of us to be more patient.

5. **What are some of the reasons why good believers have conflicts with the Almighty?** We are all human. Conflicts and errors are problematic. all conflicts are part of the human condition. We will have conflicts and misunderstandings as long as we are on planet earth. We all have different spiritual gifts and ways of expressing them. Someone else could have an accent that is difficult for us to understand. We may think that they said one thing but they said another and we reacted incorrectly to it. There are many possibilities.

6. **All of Gods people are different. Each of us have a special reason for being here. None of us are at our spiritual peak 100% of the time. Why is it that we don't have more disputes and disagreements than we do? Why do they happen?** Even when we are disobedient the LORD is still in control. It is difficult for us to believe that many of our problems in life are brought on in order for the Spirit to Shepherd us into His loving arms or to lead us in the direction that He wants us to follow?

7. **Some Believers over use a few Scripture verses and fail to study the entire Bible as they should. What do you think happens because of this?** Their life can easily become unbalanced spiritually.

8. **Another view point: How important is it that the LORD answer our prayers His way instead of our way?** Some people think that, if they can find the right group of Scripture verses, the LORD will do and answer them the way they want Him to. Humans can sometimes act very ignorantly. The Good LORD wrote the Holy Bible. We are doomed to failure if we think that we can manipulate His Scriptures so that we can have our way! Our way is not important. His way is! **But I really want it!** That is our old sin nature raising its ugly head, again!!!

9. **What is the very best thing a believer can do when he believes that the LORD answered negatively to his prayers?** It is to thank Him and praise His name. He truly knows what is best! There is nothing better than His will! We can always ask Him to help us understand His Word.

10. **What should a believer do if he is having a hard time accepting God's will?** Recognize it and confess it to the LORD. Then he should ask the LORD to help him do the things that He wants him to do and to think the thoughts that He wants him to think. And then proceed in trying to be the person that God designed you to be.

Verse	_Chapter_	_Page_	_Topic_
(Luke 14:8-11)	37	144	Seek a humble seat.

11. **What is the key element in a forgiveness prayer?** The person praying it must acknowledge his own sin and ask the only one who can truly forgive him for forgiveness. If you don't sincerely mean the prayer that you are praying, you are wasting your time.

12. **When one has unforgiven sins, what can he expect from the Master?** Corrections! Especially, if he is a believer.

13. **On a person-to-person level why should one person ask another for their forgiveness.** It is the path toward having or restoring fellowship with them.

14. **What are the differences between God's forgiveness and the forgiveness that, another person may give?** Humans tend to remember a sin that they have forgiven. Some humans will say that they forgive you but will harbor the event in their heart with a spirit of unforgiveness. God on the other hand has purposed not to remember forgiven sins.

What does a good believer normally do when he has forgiven another person of a sin that was committed against him. He will keep it in mind and will exercise care and take precautions when the forgiven person has the opportunity to re-sin.

15. **How many times should a believer forgive someone of the same sin?** As often as he asks for forgiveness.

16. **Should a believer forgive someone, even if they don't ask for forgiveness?** Yes! We should have a forgiving attitude that makes it easier for them to ask us for forgiveness. Sometimes We should tell the person that we forgive them even if they don't ask. In some cases, they may act as if they haven't done anything that needs forgiving. In that case it may be best to just drop the subject. There are some people you just can't help.

17. **Why should a believer keep on forgiving another person of repeated sins?** Scriptures state that if you don't forgive them your heavenly Father will not forgive you?

18. **Does a believer go to eternal punishment if he refuses to forgive another person of the sins that he has committed against him?** NO! But he will surely regret not forgiving him!

19. **Can another human forgive you of sin?** Only to the extent that you sinned against them. NOTE all sins are against God. All sins require His forgiveness.

20. **Are there two kinds of forgiveness?** God's forgiveness and man's forgiveness.

21. **What about sins that you have committed and are not aware of them?** The job of the Holy Spirit is to convict humans of their sins. He does His job very well. Should you sin and have no compulsion to seek forgiveness you are likely in a very terrible condition.

22. **How can you get forgiveness if the other person is now dead?** You pray sincerely to the good LORD. The possibility exists that before the person died that they may have forgiven you and was not able to let you know; but don't count on it.

23. **What should you do if you ask another person to forgive you and they refuse?** Admit that you sinned against them and beg for their forgiveness! You should pray for them and ask the LORD to lead both of you to do His will.

24. **What happens if a true believer dies just before he specifically asks another person for his forgiveness?** The good LORD is just! This is another reason to keep your forgiveness account current. There is also a tendency to sin less the more you ask for forgiveness. **NOTE: When a person becomes a believer God forgives him of all his sins, past, present, and future. Further forgiveness prayers are for the purpose of restoring fellowship with the Father!**

PRAYER PROMISES

LESSONS FROM PRAYERS THAT ARE RECORDED IN SCRIPTURE

1. **What is a prayer promise?** A prayer promise is a future action that the good LORD has already made a decision about. It is not a series of magic words that when quoted in the right order cause the LORD to do our desired actions. The LORD also does many things that are not cited in Scriptures. Most prayer promises have conditions that must be met first. Some of these conditions are included in the verse that states the promise and several are located in other parts of the Bible. The LORD is always the one in control. Not even the best believer can cause things to happen by prayer alone. The good LORD is always the one who causes, delays, or stops the actions that are prayed about. Believers should never forget that the ALMIGHTY is their loving heavenly Father!

2. **What is a common mistake that many believers make in their request prayers?** They try to tell the all-knowing all-powerful God how He should answer their prayers. I believe a simple commitment prayer that humbly asks for the LORD's

help in a matter is better received by the Master. Instead, the proud believer will describe in detail how he wants the good LORD to act in his specific circumstance. **Who knows what is best for us?**

3. **Why is it that so many requests prayed earnestly to the LORD seem to have no heavenly response?** Unconfessed sin! And an old sin nature that we allow to control us.

4. **What are the purposes of prayer promises?** They remind the believer that the good LORD is in control and that He wants to help believers by responding to their prayers. The LORD also wants believers to recognize that He is their loving heavenly Father.

5. **Can an unbeliever claim a prayer promise?** Yes. But there is little Scriptural assurance that their prayer may be answered. **UNLESS**, They are sincerely praying a salvation prayer for God to forgive them.

6. **What can a believer do if he can't find a prayer promise in the Bible that describes his perceived need?** He can still pray and ask the LORD to help him. This also applies when a believer has no idea what he needs but realizes that the good LORD can and will help a believer when the requested help is consistent with His will.

7. **If a non-believer become aware of a believer's prayer requests, what is the desired result?** That the non-believer will have his faith strengthened and eventually becomes a believer.

8. **What are some of the Scriptural requirements for a prayer request to be granted?** It must be in God's will. The person making the request should not have any unconfessed sins and has no premeditated thoughts of sinning later on.

9. **Why does the Father want to answer prayer requests?** To demonstrate His love to the believer and strengthen his faith. It is part of His fellowship time with us. In a very small way, it can be compared to times when your dog or cat is laying on the sofa next to you sleeping and you gently scratch his back. He is reminded of your presents and you are aware of his presents. It's

a good thing. Many times, His answer is geared to cause a non-believer to think positive thoughts about the LORD.

10. **What request are the least likely to be answered?** Those that do not express God's love and are outside of His will. Note: sometimes Satan will do things that we want done in order to lure the weak believes away from the Father.

Verse	*Chapter*	*Page*	*Topic*
II Chronicles 7:14	39	152	Humble prayers get answered
Psalms 91:15KJV	39	151	God rescues.
Isaiah 65:24	39	151	God answers before you ask.
Mark 11:24 KJV	39	152	Believe and receive.
Luke 11:9-10	39	151	Ask and you will revive.
John 15:7-8	39	152	Abide in Christ.

11. **Why does the Bible mention some prayers that were not answered in the affirmative?** So that believers would not get discouraged.

12. **Why do some of the prayer examples in the Bible express some attribute of the good LORD?** They serve to remind the reader about the qualities of the Almighty. He wants us to KNOW HIM!

13. **What are some of these attributes?** God loves His people, God takes care of His people, God is merciful, and God forgives sins.

14. **Why does the LORD have a bolder dramatic response to some prayers?** So that many people will come to have increased faith in Him. **Could the boldness and depth of faith of the believer have a relationship to the kind of answer that he receives?**

15. **When a good believer prays asking the Father for permission to do something that is, without question, good, Why does the good LORD sometimes say no?** Sometimes the reason is that they have done too many evil things in the past. Other times He may have selected someone else who is more skillful and who will do a much better job. It is commendable to want

to do something that is very good, but the LORD assigns the projects to whom He chooses for His own reasons. Sometimes the other believer gets the project so that he can grow spiritually.

16. **Give a dramatic example from the Bible of an answered prayer?** Elijah prayed at Carmel **I Kings 18:36-37.**

17. **What are the different components included in the LORD's prayer?** see **Matthew 6:9-13**

18. **Is there any component in the LORD's prayer that we should exclude today? Are there basic components not mentioned in it that we should include in our prayers**? Specific needs, personal needs and for others.

19. **What is the very important lesson for us that is illustrated in Jesus' prayer in Gethsemane Matthew 26:39-44?** That regardless of what we ask for, we should ask the Father to override it, if it is outside of His will! Sometimes it is necessary for us to undergo hardships. Stubbornness and pride are expensive!

20. **What lesson should we learn from the thief's prayer who was on a cross by Jesus?** See **Luke 23:42-43** – He asked for Jesus to remember him. It is never too late to pray for forgiveness and mercy as long as you are still alive. NOTE: He wasn't baptized, He wasn't in a church, He wasn't a member of a church, There is no record of him ever being in a church nor is a record of him ever hearing one of Jesus's sermons. **YET,** he believed and will be in Heaven!

Verse	_Chapter_	_Page_	_Topic_
(Genesis 18:23-33)	40	154	Abraham bargains for Sodom
(Genesis 32:24-30)	40	154	Jacob wrestles with God.
(II Samuel 7:4-29)	40	154	David was told NO!
(I Kings 8:22-54)	40	154	Solomon dedicated the temple.
(I Kings 18:36-39)	40	155	Elijah prayed at Mt. Carmel.
(II Kings 19:15-19)	40	155	Hezekiah's prayer for deliverance.
(I Chronicles 4:10)	40	155	Jabez's prayer
(I Chronicles 17:16-27)	40	155	David prays for his family.
(Nehemiah 1:4-11)	40	155	Nehemiah's prayer
(Isaiah 38:3-6)	40	155	Hezekiah prays for healing.
Ezekiel 9:8	40	156	Praying for mercy.
(Daniel 9:4-27)	40	156	Daniel prays for the captives.
(Habakkuk 3:1-19)	40	156	Habakkuk's prayer
(Matthew 6:9-13)	40	156	The LORD'S prayer
(Matthew 26: 9-13)	40	156	The LORD's prayer
(Matthew 26: 9-13)	40	157	The LORD's prayer
(Matthew 26:39-44)	40	156	Jesus prayed for God's will.

EXAMPLES OF PRAYERS OFFERED IN OUR ERA

SOMEONE ELSE'S PRE-WRITTEN PRAYERS

1. **Why do believers need to pray?** One of the most overlooked prayer needs for believers is to have fellowship with the Father. This includes asking for forgiveness, praise, thanksgiving, making request for others, and expressing our needs. When a person is in distress or hurting, it is often good when he can express it to someone who truly loves him.

2. **Why do some believer's prayers seem to be answered more often than the prayers of other believers?** Some people pray more sincerely while others try to copy the proper words or prayers that someone else used without honestly meaning what they are praying about. Few believers are fully aware of what Scripture says about prayer. They just want whatever they want and think that somehow God will provide it just because they vocalized their desire. Others sincerely repent of

their sins and ask the Father to forgive them. Then after going over their concerns ask that <u>His will is done</u>. Their prayers are answered!

3. **What is the most dramatic, miraculous answered prayer that you personally know about? (If no one has an example ask them why do they think no one has an example.)** It is not that the LORD was slack in doing His functions! He is likely waiting for a true believer to pray an answerable prayer.

4. **Why does it seem that while some very large prayers are answered and so many small less significant prayers seemingly not answered?** A casual what-ever-is -on-your-mind prayer that is not heartfelt or is spoken from a believer whose forgiveness prayers are not current should not be expected to produce very much. There is also a strong human tendency to pray simple prayers and to take for granted the results that we receive. Believers should be mindful to thank the good LORD for each answer that He chooses to give us. YES! even the small simple things that we request. Answered prayer builds faith.

5. **Who was Johann Georg Ferdinand Müller and why do you think he is mentioned in a book on prayer?** He is one of the modern day heroes of the faith. By faith he founded and paid for an orphanage and supported 50 missionaries in addition to

many other good works. He believed and read the Holy Bible and strived to follow it in every detail. There are many books about his life. I suggest "Delighted in God" as a very good starting point.

6. **Can you name any people who are serving as missionaries today? How often do you pray for them?** You should pray regularly for them and for the spreading of the gospel.

7. **Why can't ordinary believers do missionary work in their environment today?** Any believer can do "missionary "work as long as he is following the leading of the Holy Spirit. The problem is that too many people who call themselves believers are at their best lukewarm and haven't read their Bible or practiced the little they have read in the Bible! Many have not read The entire Bible even once! How can a person honestly state that they believe the Bible while at the same time they haven't completely read it, one single time?

8. **Do you know someone that you could call a "prayer warrior"?** How do you define the term "prayer warrior"? Have you ever thought of becoming one? Does anyone else think that you are

possibly one? Why not? Has anyone asked you to pray for their need?

9. **What do you think the requirements are in order for a person to be rightfully called a prayer warrior?** Live a Holy life and pray effectively for others?

10. **What do you expect to happen when you pray?** Each of us should expect changes and that God's will is done. If you don't think that you have a direct line to the Almighty, then you probably don't.

Verse	*Chapter*	*Page*	*Topic*
Exodus14:13aKJV	44	166	fear not, Seeing God's salvation
Psalms 66:18 KJV	44	167	Sin stops prayer.
Mark 11:24	44	167	Believe and receive.
(John 14:13&14KJV)	44	167	Ask in Jesus' name
John 16:24KJV	44	168	Ask and receive.
James 5:16KJV	44	166	Confession of sins
I John 3:22	44	166	Obey the LORD.
(I John 5:14KJV)	44	167	Pray according to God's will.

11. **If you were looking for a good source of pre-written prayers where would you look?** The Geneva Bible has a few very good devout prayers in it. It is a good starting place.

12. **What should you do with a good prewritten prayer?** Use it as an example of the level of piety that you should try to reach. Quoting one will not do any good unless it sincerely represents your true thoughts. **<u>There are no magic prayer words!</u>**

13. **What important factors need to be present in any prayer?** You must ask the Father to forgive you of your sins! You must sincerely mean every word of it. You need to be praying for God's will to be done, and you should spend time listening to the Spirit for His response.

14. **How would you summarizes the basic content of the LORD's Prayer?** It mentions the basic ingrediencies that should be in every prayer.

15. **What are some of the good points regarding a pre-written prayer?** Most of them are reflections of many Scripture verses. They were probably written by very devout believers.

16. **What are some of the negative points regarding a prewritten prayer?** Some people get the false impression that by vocalizing someone else's prayer that they are praying a more acceptable prayer.

17. **Is anyone familiar with Francis of Assisi's serenity prayer? There are different versions.**

   "God, grant me the serenity to accept the things
   I cannot change, Courage to change the things I
   can, And wisdom to know the difference."

   Because of translation differences some of the English versions vary. **What does this prayer illustrate?**

18. **If you fine a prewritten prayer that honestly expresses your perceived prayer needs is there any benefit in praying it instead of praying your own do-it-yourself prayer?** NOTE: There is no Scripture verses that indicate that the good LORD grades our prayers based on rules of grammar or eloquent

expression. He is concerned with heart felt content. Be honest with the Almighty. He knows our inner thoughts better than we do!

19. **How concerned do you think the good LORD is about the exact wording of our prayers?** I don't think it matters with Him. It is always proper to be respectful to the Almighty. Attitude is very important with the Father and everyone else that we meet.

20. **What do you think the important aspects, from the LORD's viewpoint, are regarding prayers?** I would suggest that how much the person believes what he is saying is very important. **The quality of the believer's faith expressed in prayers is extremely important!**

Verse	_Chapter_	_Page_	_Topic_
I Corinthians 10:13	46	17	resisting temptation

MUSICAL PRAYERS

PRAYER GUIDELINES

1. **What is the difference between a musical prayer and a good Christian Hymn?**
    There are musical standards but in a hymn's content there are a series of connected messages that generally illustrate the gospel with the last verses reflecting on the heavenly home of believer.

2. **Ask the group to name some of their favorite hymns. Is there a common thyme in their selections?**

3. **Can you name a hymn that is not a prayer?** NOTE: Prayers can express praise!

4. Ask each person to select a hymn (If hymnals are available use them) And as a group examine some of them for Scriptural content.

5. Ask the group to pick out a few hymns that end in "AMEN". What is it in them that makes them a prayer?

6. After looking at the content of several hymns, do you see prayer topics that you don't normally pray about?

7. Ask the group what is the difference between a hymn and a "Christian song". It is basically structure and content. Many so called Christian songs are sung to Worldly music. NOTE: Some of our beloved old Christian Hymns have the same music as the songs that were sung in bars and pubs.

8. Ask the group if they know of any non-Christian religion that has "congregational singing"?

9. Ask the group, if they can identify any sort of Christian gathering, where a Christian hymn is not appropriate?

10. Ask, if they know any stories behind any Christian Hymns? You can google many hymns and find the story behind the hymn; This is one of the Author's favorite hymn stories. https:// phamoxmusic.com/it-is-well-with-my-soul/#:~:text=It%20 is%20well%20with%20my%20soul%20hymn%20 is,from%20Chicago%20we%20discussed%20 above%2C%20Horatio%20Gates%20Spafford.

11. Ask the group to select a hymn and then look up the Bible verses that reflect on the thymes expressed in the hymn.

12. **What are some of the guidelines for prayer that you consider important?** You must believe what you say and ask the Father to forgive you of your sins. You can ask for anything that you want but you should always temper your prayer with the overriding request that the LORD's will is done.

13. **What do you think about quoting Scripture verses in your prayers?** Are some people who use them trying to pressure the good LORD into doing something that they want?

14. **Is there any topic not included in Matthew chapter 6 that you consider important enough to include it in your daily prayers?** The **Matthew chapter 6** prayer is general. It is also very appropriate to pray for the LORD to take care of specific personal needs.

15. **Is there anything that you shouldn't ask for in prayer?** The spiritual down fall of others, and request that are based on selfishness and greed. Anything that your old sin nature desires!

16. **After asking for forgiveness, how should you make request?** First, you should honestly state the things that you want, then you should conclude your prayer by asking that the LORD's will is done.

17. **How should you get ready for your daily special prayer?** You should select a time and a place where the distractions are at a minimum. You should begin by asking the LORD to forgive you of your sins.

18. **How is your faith strengthened by prayer?** You should pray prayers that the good LORD might choose to answer. Answered prayer builds faith!

19. **What does sin do to your prayer life?** It severely weakens it!

20. **What are the three prayers that the good LORD always answers in the affirmative?** 1. The initial forgiveness prayer where one becomes a believer. 2. The forgiveness prayers where a believer asks for forgiveness and restores his fellowship with the Father. 3. Praying that God's will is done.

CHAPTER 45

YOUR PRAYER SCORECARD

These questions are to be answered in private without any human guidance. If after answering or attempting to answer them you feel the need for additional help, you should talk with your pastor or a believer that you have confidence in and discuss the matter with them. If you for any reason don't want to do this; then, I ask you to pray about it and ask the God to have His Holy Spirit to guide you in your search for answers.

1. What have you learned about prayer?

2. Has any of your prayer's content changed as the result of this study?

3. What stands out as something that you now plan to do differently?

4. Have you noticed any differences in the outcome of your prayers?

5. Which Scripture verses now seem more important than they once did?

6. Have you changed your pattern of prayer since starting this study?

7. Has the length of your prayers changed?

8. Have you added anything to your prayers?

9. Have you subtracted anything from your prayers?

10. What are you now doing toward becoming more holy?

It is my prayer that you grow spiritually and allow the Holy Spirit to be in charge of more of your life.

Morgan Kizer

OTHER CITATIONS

1. Scanning the Plan, Dr. Kenneth F. McKinley, LeTourneau College Press 1965.
2. https://en.wikipedia.org/wiki/George_Müller
3. George Muller The man of Faith, page 8 Frederick G. Warne, Pickering & Inglis Ltd 1937.
4. George Muller Delighted in God by Rodger Steer, page 244 Harold Shaw Publishers, United Kingdom, 1981.
5. George Muller Delighted in God by Rodger Steer, Harold Shaw Publishers, United Kingdom, 1981. Page 161.
6. George Muller Delighted in God by Rodger Steer, Harold Shaw Publishers, United Kingdom, 1981. Page 226-227.
7. Transworld radio page 80 www.twrbonaire.com/about/history.html.
8. George Muller Delighted in God by Rodger Steer, Harold Shaw Publishers, United Kingdom, 1981. Page 245.
9. George Muller Man of faith and Miracles, by Basil Miller, Bethany House Publishers, 1941, page 142.
10. George Muller Delighted in God by Rodger Steer, Harold Shaw Publishers, United Kingdom, 1981. Page 302.
11. George Muller Delighted in God by Rodger Steer, Harold Shaw Publishers, United Kingdom, 1981. Page 302.
12. George Muller Delighted in God by Rodger Steer, Harold Shaw Publishers, United Kingdom, 1981. Pages 310-311.
13. *Calculated by* Michael S. Freeman, my financial advisor.
14. Page 30: From a sermon preached *by* Reverent Jason Salyer

UPCOMING BOOKS IN THIS SERIES

Praying in God's Will – This is a Scriptural based book on prayer. It cites over 200 references in both the New and Old Testaments. The Bible has much to say about prayer. It is a very important topic. This book answers many questions that believers have about prayer. Why their prayers are not answered. Which prayers are always answered. It explains how to pray. Where to pray. How often one should pray. When to decline praying and numerous details that can either harm or help an individual's prayer life. Prayer is a significant part of a believer's relationship with the Father. It discusses the things that have produced ineffective prayers.

God's Will Applications - This is a practical guide to answering many questions regarding God's will and it also provides the spiritual information and process that apply toward solving several serious problems that a believer could face during his lifetime. In one's life time there are many life changing challenges that people normally face. These are listed in the order that they may occur. Scriptures and practical advice are given so that a person in bad situations can more easily find some of the spiritual help that they will desperately need. Hopefully, by learning and understanding these principals many undesirable events can either be resolved or avoided.

Understanding God's Will - An overall detailed view of the scope and nature of God's will. God's will is the most important topic in the Universe. Understanding more of it will help the believer to better cooperate with his Heavenly Father. God's will is vast. It is concerned with everything!

Understanding God's Will Discussion Guide– A series of at least twenty questions per chapter with responses. Anyone who is a believer can lead a guided discussion Bible study by using this format. It is an excellent guide for a group Bible study based on the book "Understanding God's will". It contains additional information that is not in "Understanding God's Will". The chapter numbers and topics are the same as those in "Understanding God's Will".

God's Will at Work - This book is different from the others as it goes into the workplace. It explains the principles that produce better and more efficiently made products. It shows the reader the proven underlying Biblical principles related to productivity. These principles can expand a person's capabilities for getting their job done efficiently and successfully. Scripture tells the reader to be fruitful. This book tells you how. It illustrates that when properly applied the Holy Bible is a good foundational text book that relates to every important facet of life.

UPCOMING TOPICS (NOT YET WRITTEN)

Discovering God's Will for your life

A detailed study of Spiritual gifts. There are more of them mentioned in the Word than most believers are aware of. There may also be some spiritual gifts that are not directly mentioned in the Word. When you discover the gifts that the LORD gave you when you became a believer, then you are closer to discovering His general will for your life. When you are confident in knowing why God made you and what He designed you to do, you will be better motivated to discover and to more eagerly do more of His will.

Printed in the United States
by Baker & Taylor Publisher Services